JERKY

JERKY

The Complete Guide to Making It

MARY T. BELL

Skyhorse Publishing

Skyhorse Publishing books may be purchased in bulk at special discounts for sales promotion, corporate gifts, fund-raising, or educational purposes. Special editions can also be created to specifications. For details, contact the Special Sales Department, Skyhorse Publishing, 307 West 36th Street, 11th Floor, New York, NY 10018 or info@skyhorsepublishing.com.

Skyhorse® and Skyhorse Publishing® are registered trademarks of Skyhorse Publishing, Inc.®, a Delaware corporation.

Visit our website at www.skyhorsepublishing.com.

10 9 8 7 6 5 4 3

Library of Congress Cataloging-in-Publication Data

Names: Bell, Mary (Mary T.), author.
Title: Jerky : the complete guide to making it / Mary T. Bell.
Description: New York : Skyhorse Publishing, 2017.
Identifiers: LCCN 2016044976 (print) | LCCN 2016049629 (ebook) | ISBN 9781510711822 (paperback) | ISBN 9781510711839
Subjects: LCSH: Dried beef. | Dried foods. | Food--Drying. | Cooking (Dried foods) | BISAC: COOKING / Specific Ingredients / Meat. | COOKING / Methods / General. | COOKING / Specific Ingredients / Game. | COOKING / Methods / Canning & Preserving. | LCGFT: Cookbooks.
Classification: LCC TX749.5.B43 B448 2017 (print) | LCC TX749.5.B43 (ebook) | DDC 641.4/4--dc23
LC record available at https://lccn.loc.gov/2016044976

Cover design by Tom Lau
Cover photo credit: iStockphoto

Print ISBN: 978-1-5107-1182-2
Ebook ISBN: 978-1-5107-1183-9

Printed in China

Contents

To all grandkids, including ours: Hunter, Alysse, Oliver, and Wesley. May this collection encourage all of you to embrace the ways of our ancestors and be thoughtful, responsible stewards of our earth.

Foreword

A JERKY JUDGE

Making jerky is my hobby. It's my diversion from the courtroom. I find it satisfying and fulfilling to take a hunk of raw meat and make it tasty. Some of us make jerky because we're hunters. Not only do we want to consume what we kill, but we also prefer venison jerky to venison chops. For over thirty years, I've bow hunted deer and elk with the same loony partners and together we turned a zillion deer and twenty-three elk into jerky. With that kind of tasting experience, I think it's fair to say I've become a pretty good judge of jerky.

Jerky has become a tradition in our family. While we were students with limited income, my wife and I practically lived on wild game. Then, as well as now, she prefers her big game meat made into jerky. For three and a half decades, we've been making jerky in a food dryer and more recently we've used a smoker.

Ever notice that "he who controls food, is king"? Several years ago, I had to convince my nephew, who was doing nothing other than waiting for college to begin, to backpack with me into Idaho's mountain country for an archery elk hunt. This non-hunting six-foot-seven-inch lad from Kentucky became my pack mule, carried all my heavy camping equipment, and all he required was a slice of jerky every now and then. Like a trained seal being fed a fish, my nephew actually packed out my bull elk, with no reward other than a constant (but obscene) amount of jerky.

Some say that jerky makers are just a little off the plumb line. I make jerky for my odd assortment of wacko hunting pals, but I charge them one-third of the result—my ambulance chasing days die slowly. Once, while practicing law, I drove to Eastern Idaho to meet with a client in his home. The whole house was filled with smoke. Up above me, hanging from the rafters, were strips of raw meat. This guy had killed a deer and right there in his living room was making jerky.

Like most jerky makers, I always look forward to trying new recipes and tinkering with exotic flavor combinations. Mary Bell's earlier book *Just Jerky* became my jerky maker's bible. Not only did she teach the art of drying hamburger (which, by the way, works perfectly well with ground sausage and ground turkey), she explained how to make traditional and even unusual tasting jerkies. Mary encourages her readers to be creative and blend unusual flavors. No book on the market is better. Mary fields more questions, solves more problems, and delivers better information than anyone else in the crowded jerky theater. I know—I've appealed to her wisdom more than once. Her book is filled with great stories, more recipes for us addicts, and it's flavored throughout with good advice.

Jerky people are a goofy bunch that actually enjoy making jerky in their attics, basements, kitchens, living rooms, or garages—with or without food dryers, smokers, or ovens—and they even use such dangerous chemicals as liquid smoke. Jerky people experiment by smoking, marinating, grinding, drying, salting, and flavoring all kinds of meat. (I've made antelope and cougar jerky.) People keep searching for that one great bite of jerky that has the perfect flavor. I am personally grateful to all of those who shared their recipes, wisdom, and advice.

—**Hon. Monte B. Carlson**, Fifty Judicial District, Burley, Idaho
Editor's note: Judge Carlson passed away in 2007.

Introduction

True confession—I was once a vegetarian. In the early 1970s, I decided vegetarianism was a gentler, cheaper way for our family of three to live. We had been vegetarians about a year when my son, Eric, shouted out from the backseat of the car, "Mom I don't care if you're a vegetarian, I want a hamburger." I heard him loud and clear and drove to the nearest burger joint.

This was at the time I was putting myself through college and trying to provide good food for my two kids, Sally and Eric. We had planted a large garden and I was experimenting with various methods of preserving food. Once Eric let me know he wanted meat in our diet, I knew I had to develop the skill to bag my own and joined an archery league. One night, my archery friends brought a deer over and we butchered it at my kitchen table. I quickly learned how to cook venison and began making jerky.

As my passion for food drying grew, I sold food dehydrators at home and garden shows, fairs and sport shows. I promoted food drying in North and Central America and wrote *Dehydration Made Simple, Mary Bell's Complete Dehydrator Cookbook, Just Jerky, Jerky People*, and *Food Drying with an Attitude*. I still teach classes and talk about food drying to just about anybody who'll listen. Throughout the years, the more I learned, the more my curiosity was fueled.

In my travels, people often asked a lot of questions about how to make jerky. Is it hard? How can you tell when it's dry? What's the best marinade? Is it safe to make yourself? I learned that many people have purchased a food dehydrator just to make jerky.

If you buy a lot of jerky, if you hunt, fish, hike, or if you're just looking for a healthy low-fat snack, or you're one of those people who just took a new dehydrator out of the box and it's sitting on the kitchen counter and your kid is yelling "Dad, jerky, please!" then this book is for you.

This book is more than just instructions and recipes—it represents a community of people. Throughout these pages, you'll find people who like jerky and were willing to share their wisdom and experiences. Granted, they're all characters who like to either hunt, fish, ride horseback, canoe, sail, backpack, run a ranch, or are involved in some sort of a jerky business. "What's your story?" I'd ask them. "How did you get started making jerky? What's unique or different about how you make it?" Their answers were both fascinating and useful. Others wrote, telephoned, emailed, or connected with me through my website. "I have this really great jerky recipe," they'd say and I'd quickly jot it down. These innovative and inventive sages gave good advice and sound instructions along with some pretty terrific recipes.

You will find information on how to make jerky out of meat, fish, and poultry strips and with various ground meats. I've addressed safety concerns, as well. For a broader understanding, I included bits of history and stories from the commercial end of the jerky business.

Then, hold on to your taste buds, there are some really terrific jerky marinades, along with delicious and fun recipes to use jerky in cooking and baking. There are recipes for stew, bread, cake, frosting, and even ice cream. I've spent years collecting recipes, suggestions, tips, techniques, and ideas from a variety of sources and have dried jerky in dehydrators, smokers, woodstoves, campfires, and in various ovens.

It has been a long time since my son shouted for a burger from the backseat and, through all of these years, my determination to be self-sufficient turned into a life philosophy. Food represents our most intimate link and essential connection to the land. It's our source of health and vitality, the centerpiece of family, ethnic, and community traditions. Food reflects who we are and what we value. I believe the more we assume responsibility for our food supply and reduce our dependence on the food industry, the more we lessen our impact on this planet. Taking food from the land around us and preserving it provides us with a thoughtful alternative. Making jerky is intrinsic to this approach.

—Mary Bell

The author with her dehydrator.

Hunter with a hunk of meat and a bottle.

Our grandson Hunter Evans Gehrke was three days old when his mom and dad bundled him up, secured him in his car seat, and headed off to our place for Aunt Sal's wedding. Less than a mile from our home, a deer rammed their car. After we were all assured that no one was hurt, except the deer, and we'd assessed the damage to the car, we looked intently at this brand new little man and commented that on his first outing he already bagged a deer.

MY TAKE ON FOOD STORAGE

"It's a Good Idea!"

Throughout the years, many people have asked what I think about developing a food storage program. I believe that storing food is a good idea because it has always been and will always be a good idea. Our grandparents, many of our parents, rich or poor, regardless of where they lived, thought ahead to what they'd eat next week, next month, and even next year. Long-sightedness and survival were synonymous. Food storage was commonplace and expected. I believe that if each one of us looks back into our genetic pasts, we will find that our ancestors, regardless of where they lived, turned to jerky as a welcomed food.

If there is ever a time where our food supply, for one reason or another, has become limited, I think that having a full panty can relieve one from getting caught by fear and instead be able to embrace generosity.

KNOW THIS I am grateful for all of the wonderful people who contributed their jerky recipes and stories. I am hopeful that this collection will serve as a tribute to each one. Knowing that a recipe can be a coveted treasurer, I was delighted at how many people were willing to share. Businesses, of course, were not as disclosing with their recipes, but willingly gave tips, suggestions, and insights into their jerky world. This new, combined, and revised edition is a combination of *Just Jerky* and *Jerky People*. And I am sorry to say that some of these friends are now smiling down from jerky heaven.

Many of these jerky marinades were first taste-tested by the staff of L'Etoile, a restaurant in Madison, Wisconsin, under the guidance of Chef Gene Gowan. I really got lucky when I started buying grass-fed beef from our neighbors, Leslea and Brad Hodgson, owners of Galloway Beef. Not only did they provide most of the beef used to finesse these recipes, but Leslea also deserves credit for creating many of the jerky recipes. As lovers of their herd, the land, and being true jerky fans, Leslea used her knowledge to honor her cattle's ultimate gift.

My husband, Joe, is a great guy with a good heart. As these recipes were tested and re-tested, he kept repeating how he was the lucky one who was constantly being offered another jerky to taste-test. I am also grateful to my dear friend Ray Howe, who, at every stage, willingly gave me support and encouragement to tackle this endeavor.

What I've learned about making jerky and drying food is that not only is it a way to preserve food, but it is a language. I have witnessed how it serves as a bridge and connects people to their pasts, regardless of the color of their skin or

Jerky taste-testing.

Joe Deden, the author's husband.

place of origin. If you stop and think, somewhere back, each one of our ancestors knew the blessings of having access to dried food.

CHAPTER 1
What Is It?

Jerky has many meanings. As a verb, it relates to movement. To twitch is to jerk. A quick pull, twist, push, thrust, or throw is a jerk. An unexpected muscular contraction caused by a reflex action is a jerk. Convulsive or spasmodic movements and sudden starts and stops are known as jerks. Speech isn't without its jerks. To utter anything with sharp gasps is to jerk out.

Jerkin sounds like slang, but in the sixteenth century, it was an article of clothing—a short, close-fitting, often sleeveless coat or jacket. In more recent times, a jerkin became a short, sleeveless vest worn by women. A jerkin is also a type of hawk, the male gyrfalcon.

The noun jerker has two meanings: one is a British customs agent who searches vessels for unentered goods. One who, or that which, jerks is also known as a jerker.

My favorite movie is *The Jerk*, starring Steve Martin. However, a real jerk, the kind we've all encountered, is a person regarded as stupid, dull, maybe eccentric. Jerks—and jerkers, for that matter—can come from jerkwater towns.

Jerky is most commonly known as meat preserved by slicing it into strips and drying it in the sun, over a fire, or in a dehydrator, smoker, or oven. It's called *charqui*, pronounced "sharkey" in Spanish. In Africa, jerky is referred to as *biltong* and is generally quite thick and made with

For more inspiration, sing "Come On, Do the Jerk!" by the Miracles, or "Cool Jerk" by the Capitols, or "The Jerk" by the Larks. Then there's "Can You Jerk Like Me" by the Contours and Rodney Crowell's tell-it-like-it-is ballad "She Loves the Jerk."

ostrich, python, and impala—in other words, any available red meat protein. In Central and South America, this portable ancient food was called *tasajo*. Eventually dried meat became known as *jerky* or *jerked beef*. Caribbean cooks popularized a style of cooking that typically calls for a marinade laced with allspice, and that too is jerky.

REAL JERKY

Making jerky can be as simple as sprinkling salt and pepper onto meat, fish, or poultry strips and drying them over a smoky fire. Although that's a valid way to make jerky, this book will introduce you to a bolder dimension of flavor blending. Jerky can be like fine wine, a mingling of characteristics, some subtle, others robust.

When you make your own, you can select the quality and type of meat and choose from an almost endless combination of flavoring ingredients for marinades, brines, or dry cures. In addition, you get to determine if you want to add chemicals, preservatives, and flavor enhancers.

Then think about price. A single ounce of commercial jerky can cost more than $2. At $32 a pound, jerky is more expensive than spiny lobster from the coldest waters of Maine. However, homemade jerky is not only delicious, but it is also a better product and costs less money. A pound of fresh meat ($4 to $6), a cup of teriyaki sauce (50 cents), and a few pennies of electricity transforms into 6 to 8 ounces of fabulous homemade jerky.

I think it's fair to say that many of us were first introduced to jerky via an in-store purchase. According to a 2015 Nielsen report, the popularity of jerky continues to soar. ". . . meat snack sales (which include jerky and sticks) have risen from $1.7 billion in 2010 to $2.5 billion in 2014." The market demand for meat snacks has been explosive, making it the fastest growing segment of the snack food industry.

A quick check of a store-bought jerky label will list ingredients that often include water, salt, corn syrup, dextrose, spices, smoke flavoring, monosodium glutamate (MSG), sodium erythorbate, garlic powder, sodium nitrate, BHA, BHT, potassium sorbate, and citric acid. Commercial jerkies are made from either strips or formed ground meats with textures that vary from hard and tough to moist and tender.

Jerky is most commonly made from dried and flavored raw meat, but can be made from fresh, frozen, canned, or even luncheon meats such as pepperoni, venison sausage, ham, salami, pastrami, smoked turkey, and chicken breasts. Originally, *venison* meant any game, but today it's synonymous with deer meat but actually includes elk, moose, antelope, and reindeer. Many critters have been turned into jerky, including kangaroo, rattlesnake, ostrich, mountain sheep, whale, ducks, geese, blue gills, smelt, carp, beef, buffalo, rabbit, lamb, goat, chicken, turkey, emu, sole, flounder, halibut, tuna, rock cod, sunfish, crappies, perch, walleye, bass, salmon, trout, and catfish. Liver, heart, and even blood has been used to create jerky.

Blood Jerky

In times of scarcity, even blood was dried and stored. In Reay Tannahill's book *Food in History*, a French traveler noted that seventeenth-century Irish peasants ". . . bled their cows and boiled the blood with milk and butter from the same beast." Then they added a mixture of savory herbs and considered this to be one of their most delicious dishes. "In the counties of Tyrone and Derry, blood was preserved by allowing it to coagulate in layers, each layer was strewn with salt until a little mound formed, then it was cut in squares and stored."

THE HISTORY OF DRYING

Humans have benefited from dried foods since the Cro-Magnon era. Our ancestors responded to the same hunger we feel and needed to eat and feed their families just like us. Early people observed and copied the natural drying process. Animals were cached in trees and left to dry in the sun and wind. Dried grasses, seeds, fruits, and nuts were gathered and stored. The sun, wind, and smoke from fires served as methods of preservation by removing water from food.

For centuries, dried meat and salted fish, along with bread and beans, have been staples. Archaeological digs have provided clues about our ancestors' diet. They have presented evidence of dried bison, elk, deer, antelope, wolves, coyotes, badgers, beaver, fox, rabbits, squirrels, salmon, catfish, cod, perch, carp, prairie chickens, grouse, geese, turtles, and snakes. Humans have long recognized the value of camping near the sea, lakes, rivers, and streams. Shellfish, crustaceans, and sluggish fish were netted, harpooned, or scooped by hand. Long before the luxury of electricity, fish were salted and sun-dried on riverbanks. Stored grains, berries, and meats kept people alive throughout the year.

Worldwide dried fish continues to be a principal food source. With approximately 27,300 species of fishes, it's clear why they've been called "the wheat of the sea."

As pioneers spread westward, they relied on a Native American staple called *pemmican*. This became a mainstay as the West was settled. This high-protein, calorie-rich, concentrated, portable food was made by combining powdered or finely chopped dried meat, dried berries, and melted animal fat (bone marrow was preferred) and then mixed it into a thick paste and stuffed into airtight animal skins. This survival food was used by the Arctic explorers Admiral Robert E. Peary and Admiral Richard E. Byrd and served as an important World War I survival ration.

After a hunt, fresh meat was brought to camp, cut into strips, and dried over the warm circulating air of a campfire. When dry, it was packed in skin bags called *parfleches*. Bones were boiled and the fat marrow was kept in a bladder to use to make pemmican.

Partially dried fish fillets were placed on sheets of birch bark and then mashed smooth. Maple sugar was added to sweeten and serve as a preservative. Salmon was dry cured or soaked in brine and then smoked over an alderwood fire or dried in the sun. For centuries, cleaned fish and meat were packed in crocks of salted water. (A brine drew moisture out of the soaking food and the salt replaced water.) Once brining was completed, the liquid was drained off and the fish or meat was ready to be dried.

Today, we air-dry food by placing it in direct or indirect light so that dry, warm air can circulate around and through it. The more air movement, the faster drying can happen. You can place food on screens placed high above campfires, but you could also put it on cookie sheets or baking racks and place near heat registers, on radiators, near warm refrigerator air exhaust, or on sun-warmed rocks, in car windows, and even laid on flat rooftops. Clotheslines and fishing lines can be been strung up with meat and fish strips where hot air circulates. They can be hung with clothespins, or pierced with hooks, rods, wire, or hangers and draped over hot, rising air. Creative folks have even utilized the hot radiating air from their woodstove to make jerky.

When drying jerky outdoors, the meats must be brought inside or tightly covered at night to prevent them from absorbing nighttime dew. Drying jerky outdoors can be difficult because you cannot control the temperature—not to mention dirt and insects, which can present more than a few problems.

The Drying Stage

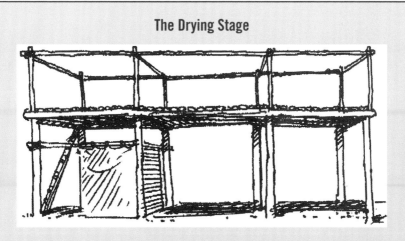

One of my all-time favorite books is *Buffalo Bird Woman's Garden*, which is about how Buffalo Bird Woman, of the Hidatsa tribe, lived along the Missouri River and planted, harvested, and preserved food. Drying meat, fruit, and vegetables was extremely important and each community had a drying stage. The stage was a place of respect and honor because it supported their way of life.

Each summer, cottonwood timbers were cut, the bark was peeled, and the posts were left to dry throughout the winter. In late spring, the men raised the heavy posts and the forks used to support the floor beams. Then the women built the thirty-foot-long and twelve-foot-wide platform floor. Poles about two inches thick by thirteen feet long, called *drying rods*, were placed so that their ends projected over each rail end. Then on sunny, windy days, strips of raw meat were hung on these rods and dried in forty-eight to seventy-two hours. Sometimes a low, smoky fire was lit under the stage floor to speed up the drying process.

DRYING FISH

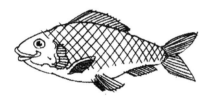

While researching the history of drying fish, I found that almost every kind of fish has been dried throughout time and in almost every corner of the world. However, fresh fish begin to deteriorate the moment they leave water, especially in hot, humid weather. To overcome the perishability problem, fish were either coated with salt or soaked in a heavily salted brine. Most dried fish was never intended to be eaten as jerky and required soaking before use in cooking.

Fish was dried in the sun and wind, hung over smoky fires, strung on hooks, suspended from poles, lay on bamboo racks, or placed on hot flat rocks. Big fish were filleted and de-headed, leaving the collarbone to hang to dry. Medium-sized pieces took about three days to air-dry and larger pieces took more than a week.

When selecting fish for drying, always choose fresh fish that have bright, shiny, bulging eyes, pink or red gills, smooth scales that are tight against the body, and no disagreeable odor. The flesh should be firm and spring back when touched.

Frozen fish can be used to make jerky and, when thawed, will absorb flavorings faster because the cell structure was broken. Generally, fish are filleted and deboned and the skin is removed, but when I dry smelt, I do not remove the skin. I remove the scales of lake trout, but leave the skin on. Fish is more delicate than meat and absorbs flavor easier and dries faster.

Throughout the jerky-making process, cleanliness and sanitation are very important. Rinse fish in fresh, clean, cool water. Cut fillets into ¼-inch-thick, ½-inch-wide strips that are 3 to 4 inches long. Making slashing cuts crosswise into the flesh helps flavors penetrate.

To keep your house from smelling like fish, you can, after your dehydrator is loaded, set it in the garage, but make sure it is sheltered from any strong winds. If oil beads up, pat it off before packaging it.

I'd been trying to make a good-tasting fish jerky to eat as lightweight, high-protein snack for years, but until I understood it didn't need as much salt as was called for in many traditional brine/marinade recipes, I'd been unsuccessful.

It is also true that, as a Midwesterner, I was not as familiar with preserving fish and compensated for my inexperience by touring several fish smokehouses. I had the good fortune to talk with skilled fisherpersons who had firsthand experience drying bluegills, smelt, carp, catfish, crappies, perch, trout, salmon, red snapper, sea bass, tuna, and more. After applying what I'd learned about drying other meat, and by reducing the salt, my fish jerky tasted absolutely delicious.

LUTEFISK—JERKY BY ANOTHER NAME

Traditionally, dried cod was bathed in a lye-based brine and was heavily salted. Dried cod, also known as lutefisk, has been considered a miracle food because just a few servings has fed extremely large crowds.

To eat lutefisk, wash in cold water and soak overnight in clean cold water. While soaking, it can develop a gelatinous consistency. Drain and put in a glass or enamel pan (not aluminum) and bake at 400 degrees for 20 minutes. Serve with lots of pepper and butter.

CHAPTER 2
Equipment

When air is heated, it becomes dry. Circulating dry air can be used to eliminate water in food. Best conditions allow for airflow to evenly distribute throughout a drying chamber, otherwise the intended jerky may need to be turned over every few hours so that all surfaces receive the impact of the dry air.

For making jerky safely, the USDA Meat and Poultry Hotline currently recommends you "heat meat to 160 degrees and poultry to 165 degrees before the dehydrating process." After reaching that temperature a constant temperature of 130 to 140 degrees must be maintained during the drying process. The USDA requires this because the drying process must be fast enough to dry the meat before it spoils and must remove enough water that microorganisms cannot grow.

ELECTRIC DEHYDRATORS

My first choice of equipment for making jerky is an electric dehydrator. Most dehydrators have a thermostat that makes it possible to control the drying temperatures and a fan to push the heated air throughout the drying chamber. Electric dehydrators can be used anytime, day or night, rain or shine—just turn it on, set the temperature, and within a few hours, you've got jerky.

Electric food dehydrators vary in size and style and can range in price from $20 to more than $300. They can be round, square, or rectangular. Square or rectangular dehydrators resemble microwave ovens or mini fridges and have front doors and removable trays. The heat source and fan are usually on the back or on one side. Round dehydrators have a heat source and fan either on the top or bottom and trays that stack one on top of another.

How long it will take to make jerky in a dehydrator will depend on the size of the meat strips, moisture content, temperature, amount of humidity in the air, number of trays, and wattage of the dehydrator. I use a 1,000-watt dehydrator and set the temperature between 145 and 160 degrees. Generally, eight trays of ground meat jerky will take 6 to 8 hours to dry and eight trays of strip jerky will take 8 to 10 hours.

If you have a dehydrator that does not have a temperature control, you can still use it, but first put your jerky in a 160-degree oven for at least 10 minutes. You can use a meat thermometer with a stainless steel point to check the internal temperatures of drying meat.

Dehydrator Accessories

Most dehydrators have accessories that enhance the drying process. One accessory is called a *mesh* or an *insert sheet*. These sheets have smaller holes than a dehydrator tray and thereby help minimize dripping from one tray to another, keep food from sticking, and make cleanup easier.

Another accessory, called either a *roll-up* or *leather sheet*, is a solid plastic tray liner that, like the mesh sheet, fits inside a drying tray. Although these sheets are primarily used for drying puréed foods, such as fruit or vegetable leathers, they come in handy when drying fatty meat because they block oil or any other liquids from dripping down from one tray onto another.

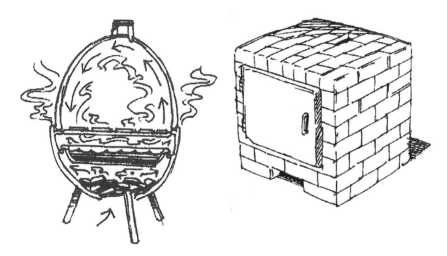

SMOKERS

Smoking is a preservation method that dates back to when humans first made fire. Perhaps our attraction to smoked foods is instinctive, if not genetic, and may be why so many jerky recipes call for liquid smoke.

Smoky air is dry air. It removes water, adds flavor, has a preservative effect, and helps seal in natural flavors. According to the late Dr. Art Maurer, professor in the department of poultry science at the University of Wisconsin–Madison, when smoke accumulates on the surface of jerky, it becomes a film or protective barrier that has an antioxidant effect that helps slow the development of rancidity, oxidation deterioration, and bacterial growth.

Smokers are metal containers designed to confine smoke. They have a heat source where burnable items, mainly in the form of chips, shavings, chunks, or sawdust are allowed to smolder and thereby create smoky air. Smokers have trays, racks, or hooks to hold strips that allow smoke to swirl up and go through drying meat. Smokers have top or bottom drafts that help circulate dry air throughout the entire container.

A smoker can cost as little as $30 and go up from there. When using a commercial smoker, follow the manufacturer's directions, because each one can have its own quirks. Smokers can be as simple as erecting a metal foil tent over a hibachi or using a metal drum, or be as elaborate as a state-of-the-art brick smokehouse. With a little creativity, time, and patience you can make a smoker that will provide you with tasty and inexpensive jerky.

The smoke produced from various woods can change the color and taste of jerky. Hickory is the most commonly used wood, especially with red meat and poultry, because it adds a hearty flavor. Mesquite burns hot, but can turn meat bitter if smoked too long. Alder's delicate flavor is great with salmon. Apple and cherry add a slightly sweet, fruity taste to chicken and turkey. Pecan, a mellow version of hickory, burns cool.

In addition to using wood to produce smoke, you can burn fresh or dried herbs, orange or lemon peels, grapevines—even corncobs add flavor and interest. Our local butcher, Willie Cambern, made great jerky at his grocery store in Fountain, Minnesota. He combined equal portions of hickory and maple chips. He thought hickory alone created a bitter taste, but with the addition of maple, his jerky tasted sweeter and had a red, shiny coat.

Smokers are used outside, so pay attention to the wind, as it may impact the drying process. Keep long-handled tongs and oven mitts handy and be careful—both the outside and inside of a smoker can get hot.

Wet wood produces more smoke and smolders better than dry wood, so before starting the smoking process, soak wood chips or sawdust in water. Place marinated strips in single layers so the smoky air can circulate freely around all surfaces. If the smoker is not producing enough smoke and the fire is dying, check the air holes and open the vents to let in additional oxygen. Close the vents if the temperature gets too hot.

Vince Deden smoking meat.

If a smoker is the only method of drying you're using, it can take six to twelve hours of continuous smoking to get strips dry. My father-in-law, Vince Deden, would sometimes get venison jerky smoked and dried in about eight hours. When smoking jerky for a long time, you will need to resupply your smoke source.

How long it will take to smoke jerky depends on the thickness of strips, quantity of smoke, and amount of meat being processed, as well as altitude, wind, cold or rainy weather, and humidity.

When relying on a smoker for the main drying method, you can pre-dry strips in an oven or a dehydrator. I use smoking as the last stage in the jerky making process in conjunction with my electric food dryer. I have found that smoke adheres to a dry surface better than a wet one. I put wet jerky strips in my dehydrator and, when almost dry, I transfer them to a smoker to finish the process.

OTHER TYPES OF DRYING

Ovens

Even though you can use an oven to make jerky, I have found it difficult to maintain a constant temperature of 160 degrees. The lack of airflow complicates matters. If the heat is too high, it can cause jerky to become tough, taste burnt, and be brittle. Depending on the size and thickness of the drying meat, temperature, and the type of oven, making jerky in an oven can take two to twenty-four hours.

Because marinated strips can be drippy, line the oven floor with aluminum foil or place a cookie sheet or a cake pan on the bottom shelf to help make cleanup easier. Lay marinated strips crosswise over the oven racks, or spear the strips with shower or drapery hooks or shish-kabob sticks hung from the oven bars or laid across the oven racks with the strips hanging down. If strips are spread out on a cookie sheet, during the drying process it will be necessary to turn the pieces over every hour so the drying air can reach all sides.

If your oven does not cycle below 200 degrees, prop the oven door open about an inch by inserting a non-burnable item, like a low-powered fan, in the opening. Watch carefully so the fan doesn't move or get too hot. Also keep an eye (and ear) on any smoke detectors and fire alarms while propping the oven door. When using a gas oven, be careful the fan does not blow out the pilot light. Another option to maintain temperatures between 150 to 165 degrees is to turn the oven off and on while monitoring the temperature.

Microwave

Microwave ovens are designed to heat and cook food quickly, but not to remove water from food. Over the years, I have tried to make jerky in a microwave, but I have never created a jerky that compared to what I can make in a dehydrator. My microwave jerky was always overcooked and crisp. If you choose to experiment with using a microwave, I suggest you vary the power and keep a close eye on what's happening.

Convection

Convection ovens circulate air and can be used for making jerky. If you have a convection oven or you are considering buying one, contact the manufacturer and ask that they provide you with information on how best to use it. Then expect to do some experimenting.

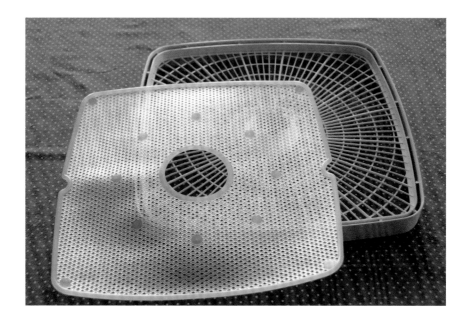

CHAPTER 3
Jerky Business: The Commercial Side

Jerky is big business, with sales increasing each year. In 2000, the US Snack Food Association reported that meat snack sales reached $1.74 billion. Today, the jerky market has ballooned into a multibillion dollar industry. Sales have risen 13 percent since 2013, up 46 percent since 2009. The Link Company, the largest jerky maker in America, sells more than $1 billion in meat snacks each year. In January 2015, the industry research firm IBIS World reported, "The meat jerky industry's small-scale nature, relatively low prices, and innovative flavors and content have led revenue to grow . . . to $1.1 billion in the last five years." The 2019 "revenue is forecasted to continue growing, albeit at a slightly slower rate of 1.7 percent per year."

Dean Clark, founder of HI Mountain Spice Company, pointed out that these figures do not include the money spent by jerky makers on jerky-making supplies. For example, Cabela's, a large outfitter, offers a variety of jerky-making supplies that include dehydrators, smokers, cures, jerky guns and shooters, meat grinders and slicers, wood chunks, oven accessories, vacuum packers, spices, cures, and thank goodness, books. I interviewed jerky makers to get the scoop on their jerky businesses.

Jessica Ellenbecker's store, All Things Jerky.

ALL THINGS JERKY

Jessica Ellenbecker is a feisty gal who saw the jerky world opening up and decided to jump in with her business, All Things Jerky.

As the company's head jerkologist, Jessica said, "For as long as I can remember, I've loved jerky. Every car trip our family took, we always snacked on jerky. My father was a hunter, so I grew up eating lots of venison, rabbit, squirrel, and even porcupine."

Then as destiny would have it, Jessica stumbled upon a store that primarily sold jerky. "I was in heaven," she recalled. "From then on, all I could think about was opening a store in my hometown of Appleton, Wisconsin."

Her goal was to provide quality jerky and stock the supplies people would need to make their own. "When people come into our store, we want them to have a complete jerky experience, so we offer samples. Each customer can customize their own bag of jerky with flavors of their choosing. We want people to be excited with what we consider the best jerkies."

Most of Jessica's products come from small to midsized companies, with an emphasis on local suppliers. "We do not sell 'gas station' or mass-produced jerky," she said proudly. "People are looking for small batch, better-quality jerky." She said, "Gourmet and exotic flavors are on the rise, like, sriracha honey. People are looking for something unique and tasty. Alligator and kangaroo are our most popular exotics. Buffalo and elk are gaining in popularity due to their health value. We try to stay in front of the trends by offering our customers products before they become popular."

GENTLEMAN JIM'S QUEST

This is the story of Gentleman Jim and his desire to make and sell his own jerky. It provides an example of the challenges involved in making a jerky business happen. It was no easy trick!

After watching guys sell "nickel bags" of jerky on the street corner, Jim McGrew decided to give it a whirl. Then after spending $22,000 for equipment and receiving an education in the ways of governmental bureaucracy, his dream finally came true and he got his United States Department of

Agriculture (USDA) approval to run a manufacturing plant. Gentleman Jim made a spicy, a sweet, a regular, a teriyaki, and pepper jerky.

His adventure into the jerky world began when a buddy gave him a dehydrator. "When I took it out of the box, I found a recipe for jerky, bought a pound of meat, followed the directions, and shared it with my sailing crew. Ever since that day I was expected to bring jerky every time we raced our Morgan 30 sailboat, *Jackal*," he recalled. "Human movement can be a critical factor in winning or losing a race, so once the sails get trimmed and the boats up to speed, we adjusted each crew member's position to get the maximum speed and after that the crew couldn't get up and move around. That meant everyone got pretty hungry during a thirty-mile race, but with a few sticks of jerky in their pockets, the guys had a great high-protein food readily available."

With friends and racing buddies urging him to sell his jerky, Jim called the USDA to find out what he needed to do to establish a business.

"You've got to have a licensed kitchen," he was told. "Each facility is different and requires individual attention."

He went to the Department of Agriculture's website, drew up a business plan, and began to design his processing area. After filing the necessary papers, he applied for a permit. He secured a space for his facility and put up new white walls and added new countertops, then he put in a floor drain and stainless steel sinks. With his operating and sanitation plan in hand, he called his local inspector to see if he had everything in order. The inspector advised him to ask other jerky producers for their assistance.

"I called a local jerky guy, explained who I was, and told him what I was trying to do," Jim said.

"Do you get your labels approved?" the guy asked.

"What? By whom?" Jim mumbled. Jim had designed, printed, and paid for five thousand labels only to find that they should have been approved first. He had no choice but to toss those labels in the garbage. Five jerky flavors meant five labels and five different approvals with the percentages of each ingredient listed and a nutritional analysis, including the moisture content. Then he had to submit proposed sketches of each label.

The next step was to get his Hazard Analysis and Critical Control Points (HAACP) plan approved. The plan outlines the production process from start to finish, covering what procedures are required to prevent contamination and analyzing where and how a product is likely to be contaminated by microorganisms, pathogens, foreign objects, spoilage, and much more. Jim was required to track everything, from receiving the raw meat all the way through shipping. He had to record the temperature inside of the delivery truck, what time the beef was received at his plant, what time the meat was put in the cooler, the marinade time, the beginning of the drying process and again when it was packaged. He had to document how often he calibrated each thermometer. Batch numbers had to be assigned. He had to have a procedure for noting any problems, how they were solved, and what was changed so the problems would not be repeated.

Jim persisted and found other models on the USDA website. He adjusted his plan and again called the inspector.

Once again the inspector was impressed with the facility, but deemed it not ready. Then Jim installed foot-level operating pedals on his three sinks ($400 each), put in a bathroom fan, and used foam to seal off all the pipes running through the building to prevent any bug infestation.

"I'd had enough," Jim recalled. "I told the inspector I wanted my license!"

Finally, he'd cleared all the hoops and passed inspection. Then, each week he bought as much as one thousand pounds of fresh London broil (top round) beef. "I like the way top round holds up in a marinade," Jim said. He single-handedly sliced about fifty pounds an hour. "No machine will ever cut it," he said emphatically. "I like the rugged look of hand-sliced jerky." Jim chopped fresh onions, mashed fresh garlic, and used the highest-quality seasonings. He used no other preservative in his marinades other than those in soy sauce. Each batch of marinated slices was put in tubs and refrigerated for twenty-four hours. He spread the strips out on his dehydrator trays and, after about six hours, his jerky was ready. He let it cool, weighed it, and vacuum-packed it in four-ounce bags and then attached a label.

"Creating and getting my plan approved ended up being the most daunting task I'd ever undertaken," Jim recalled after pulling everything together. He also now understands why guys sell bags of jerky on the street.

His advice to make good jerky is this: always use good-quality meat and ingredients and do not be afraid to experiment.

OAK MEADOW MEATS

One sunny spring Saturday morning, Leslea Hodson and I went to our neighboring town of Harmony, Minnesota, to talk with Mike and Vanessa Aggen, owners of Oak Meadow Meats. Mike, a former meat inspector for the state of Minnesota, and Vanessa, a marketing professional, decided to move back from the big city to the little southeastern Minnesota town of Harmony and invest in a local butcher shop.

Even though this couple had experience with the licensing rules, they too found the process numbing, to say the least. Through a lot of work and patience, they were eventually able to appease the MDA and get their business up and running. In our little part of the world, Oak Meadow has become known for its outstanding line of beef strip jerkies.

Mike explained how they make jerky: "We start with 50 pounds of choice inside round. Then we cut with the grain and make 1-inch slabs ⅜ inches thick. To do this, we use a Bird Sir Steak slicer. After marinating one week in the cooler, the strips are racked on jerky screens and put in an Enviro-Pak Smokehouse. The smokehouse goes through a five-stage drying process where temperatures range from 125 to 170 degrees. Hickory sawdust is automatically fed into the burning chamber. After four and a half hours, the jerky is left to cool overnight to bring the moisture back. This helps create a jerky that is easier to chew. With this process, enough moisture is left in the jerky that it must be kept in a refrigerator or freezer."

THE COST OF INVENTION

Sean Broadnax, a tenacious Irishman from northern California, invented a Mother's 2-Hour Jerky Maker. His story reveals what it takes to fully develop an idea all the way and make it pay. His 14½-inch long, 8-inch wide Teflon-coated, aluminum jerky maker had holes in its folding top for seven skewers intended to hold marinated meat strips.

Sean got the idea for his clever gadget in a flash. A friend of his told him how her mother had made beef jerky outdoors by hanging it on a line. Instantly, he imagined a metal rack he could use to make jerky in an oven. After that, he became obsessed with recreating the image. "Since that first day, I was married to this product," he confessed. He got busy and

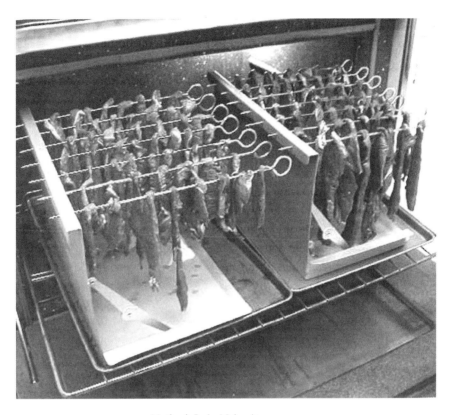

Mother's Jerky Maker in an oven.

experimented with numerous batches of jerky to see how his jerky maker could be improved. After poking marinated strips with skewers and locking each one in a hole, the strips hung straight down over the catch pan. The loaded jerky maker was put in a 200-degree preheated oven.

"Then I got excited thinking about how much money I was going to make," he chuckled. "I thought success would happen in a matter of months, but I was in for a big surprise."

To protect his invention, he paid a patent marketing company $10,000. Sean shook his head. "If I ever do anything like this again, I'll hire a patent attorney."

Sean worried about where the money would come from to pay for everything, marketing and improving his invention, how to create the necessary artwork, making label decisions, developing user instructions, deciding which recipes to use, and how to create the right packaging. Plus everything cost more than he thought. He anxiously wondered whether people would like and use his invention.

Thinking he had his ducks in a row, Sean sat down, turned on his TV, and "tears of pain rolled from my eyes as I watched Ron Popeil make beef jerky in a dehydrator. I was shattered!" he recalled. "I thought it was over, and for six months I never mentioned the word *jerky*." Then a friend gave him an instruction manual for Popeil's dehydrator. "I read in the manual that it took ten to twelve hours to make jerky. I got excited because my invention took only two hours. I was back in business!"

Through all of this, Sean lived in his mother's garage and manufactured jerky makers. He sold eighty jerky makers at the Yuba-Sutter County Fair and, after that, things started to click. A kitchen distributor marketed it to California stores. Then an infomercial company promoted it. After a decade of dedication, his business started to pay off. His voice cracked: "It was the craziest time. Mom was there for me through it all. Then cancer took her." He paused. "Sometimes I wonder what was the real cost of trying to make this happen."

THE JERKY KING

Art's father, Constantino, an Italian immigrant, founded the Oberto Company in Seattle in 1918. Today, it's the second largest producer of beef jerky in the nation, with more than four hundred varieties of dried meat products. As of July 2014, the company reported an annual revenue of $220 million.

Art Oberto dons the title Jerky King and owns a "jerky mobile." Art recalled one night while at home watching television with his wife, Dorothy, that he saw the Batmobile and said, "If they can have one, we can have one, too." Since then, Art has turned several Lincoln Town Cars into jerky mobiles and, without a doubt he has been OH BOY! OBERTO'S number one cheerleader.

Art, a natural-born entrepreneur, claims "Have fun!" as his motto. Wearing a white suit with a red, white, and green OH BOY! OBERTO tie, Art drives his jerky mobile around the Seattle, Washington, area promoting the company. "You've got to do things because you enjoy them," he said. This philosophy has made Art and the Oberto business very successful.

From cars to hydroplanes: Oberto sponsored the *Miss Madison* hydroplane based in Madison, Indiana, from 2000–2015.

Art was sixteen when his dad died and, after that, he helped his mother keep the business alive by riding his bike and delivering Italian sausage. As the business grew, they developed jerky, sausage sticks, smoked dinner sausages, dry salami, kippered beef, and pickled sausage. By 1995, the company had doubled its sales, employing more than 800 people with four plants covering 275,000 square feet of manufacturing and warehousing space.

According to Art, "Jerky's popularity skyrocketed when people realized that it's a good source of protein. At one time, beef had a bad rap, but that image changed. Then we got lucky and had the right products at the right time."

Although Oberto marinades are corporate and family secrets, Art said they start the jerky process by using top round cuts. After the beef is trimmed, it is sliced about one-quarter-inch thick and then marinated for twenty-four hours. It is then either air-dried or placed on screens and then dried and smoked. "Careful attention is paid to the temperature and humidity. Each flavor has its own set formula," Art said. "If you take the same identical piece of meat and vary the temperature or the humidity, or change one marinating ingredient, it will taste different."

Art said their business success was based on producing the best possible products, making the numbers come out right, and having happy, contented employees who are responsive to customers. "They will tell you what they want. They might want a jerky that's softer or one that's hotter, so remember to listen. When these things are taken care of, everything else will take care of itself."

Then he advised, "Regardless of what business you are in, find at least one mentor. My mentors helped me stay in business." He recalled how, over the years, he heard his mentors repeatedly say, "Time is your most important commodity. Get the job done. Think lazy. Don't do more than you have to." He chuckled. "I loved that advice; it made my life and my work much more fun."

"Do you plan to retire?" I asked.

"I don't need to," he chuckled, "I've never had a job. I've always had hobbies."

THE JERKY LINK

ORDINARY PEOPLE DOING THE EXTRAORDINARY is on the sign at the entrance of the Link Snack headquarters and plant/processing facility in Minong, Wisconsin. "Everyone works hard," CEO Jack Link said. "Our success is a result of employee loyalty and a lot of hard work, soap, and water." For years, the Link Company has been a major nationwide jerky supplier to convenience, grocery, and drug stores.

The Link Company is another family-owned and managed business where sons followed in their dad's footsteps. Is it something about cutting meat, or wanting to work hard, or is it family loyalty?

Chris Link, Jack's grandfather, settled in Minong in the 1890s, worked on the railroad, and bought and sold cattle. "Grandpa had a sixth sense for cattle," Jack said. "In a split second, he could pick out the best." Chris's son, Earl, operated a stock farm, owned a feed, grocery, and hardware store, and also ran a meat market. Wolf, Earl's brother, went out west to buy horses until 1938 and then became one of the biggest Allis-Chalmers machinery dealers in the country. In 1972, he built a meat-packing plant and processed about 550 cows per day and, by the mid-eighties, was supplying McDonald's with meat.

One fall day, Jack and his sons, Troy and Jay, were going hunting when they stopped at a convenience store and bought jerky. Throughout the day, they gnawed on that tough jerky. Then a light bulb went on—with their family knowledge of meat processing and sausage-making, they believed they could make a moister and a tenderer jerky.

In 1984, after submitting their first package of jerky to the USDA, they were told it could not be called jerky because of its high moisture content. In time, the USDA gave them permission to call their new meat snack *kippered beef steak.*

"Most convenience store operators didn't know what *kippered* meant and thought it meant fish," Jack said. Eventually, consumers loved it and demanded more flavors. Within a few years, they had a multimillion-dollar snack food business. The Link Company does more than $1 billion in sales annually and dominates a jerky market they helped create. The brand's popularity was cemented with its easily recognized red, black, and white labels and its slapstick advertisements featuring a jerky-loving Sasquatch.

Like KFC's Colonel Sanders, the Link Company is protective of its recipes, but recommended that jerky makers use the freshest and highest-quality ingredients they can get their hands on.

A FOUNTAIN OF JERKY CREATIVITY

Dean Clark, past president and founder of Hi Mountain Jerky (now Hi Mountain Seasonings), deserves a gold star for being a fountain of creativity. He's got spices, a knife that slices, and even a board to hold raw meat while slicing.

Dean got his start in the world of meat while working behind the counter of his father's meat market in California's San Fernando Valley. Then, after working in the oil business, he got into the restaurant business, developed Chef's Seasonings, and marketed under the Campfire label.

By 1991, the spice line was well-positioned for the beginning of the homemade jerky craze. It was the same time when women discovered that jerky was a high-protein, low-fat snack. Dean predicted the growth of sales due to the addition of jerky to the product line in supermarkets, drugstores, mass-market retailers, gasoline and convenience stores, military commissaries, and select club and dollar retail chains. By the end of 2014, dried meat snacks sales exceeded $2.6 billion.

"Jerky is a perfect food," he said. "It's nutritious and easy to stash in a saddlebag." He asked, "Know why it's called jerky? It's because raw meat was cut with the grain—not against it—so when it is dry you have to yank or rip it." Dean recalled, "Old-timers used leather straps from their saddles, or buggy harness straps or two leather belts, as a guide to cut the fresh, raw meat to get a uniform thickness."

Dean cuts eye of round into one-quarter-inch-thick strips, then weighs it and measures the seasonings. He liberally sprinkles seasoning on each piece so that all surfaces are covered. His dry cure contains salt, sugar, flavorings and, other than sodium nitrite, does not use chemicals or preservatives. He puts the strips in a sealable plastic bag or a nonmetal airtight container and marinates it in the refrigerator for twenty-four hours.

Dean's tips include: "Think ahead. The market's out there." And, "You've got to have a scale to make jerky," he said. "You must weigh the meat to accurately add spices." Then he added, "When using a dry cure as a marinade, first dissolve the seasonings in ice water." And lastly he commented, "Meat absorbs a marinade better when it's a little dry."

Making It!

Making jerky engages the senses—you taste test the marinade, smell the jerky as it dries, feel its texture to test for dryness, rely on sight to judge its longevity, and then your taste buds get a thrill.

Jerky is most often defined as raw meat that's been flavored and then dried. It can be in the form of strips or ground meat (like hamburger) flavored with a marinade, brine, or a dry cure. In addition, jerky can be made from cooked or processed meats like ham, salami, and chorizo.

The USDA recommends drying at a temperature of 160 degrees. When I wrote the book *Just Jerky*, the late Dr. Art Maurer, professor in the department of poultry science at the University of Wisconsin–Madison, said, "Meat must be dried in an environment capable of maintaining a temperature of at least 145 degrees with its internal temperature remaining at that temperature for at least 30 minutes."

If your drying equipment does not have a temperature control, you can pre-dry the intended jerky in a 160-degree oven for 20 minutes. If you do pre-dry jerky in an oven, it's not as important to maintain a high temperature during the drying process.

> **Good Idea**
>
> The first couple of times you make jerky, start with small batches until you're thrilled with your results.

When concocting a marinade, stop to smell and taste as you add each ingredient and make adjustments. After mixing the ingredients together, allow 15 minutes for flavors to blend before adding the strips or ground meat. As a rule of thumb, I generally use about one cup of liquid for strips and no more than half a cup with ground meat.

I like to use marinating containers with tight-fitting lids. Self-sealing plastic bags also work well because, during the marinating process, you can pick up the bag, move the meat around, and help it receive the full benefit of the marinade.

Good Idea

BBQ jerky clearly labeled with masking tape.

After putting meat in a marinade, write the name of the jerky on a strip of masking tape and attach it to the marinating container. After removing the meat from that container, transfer that same label to the drying trays. When the jerky is dry, put that same label on its new storage container.

Marinating time can vary from a few minutes to days. That said, when marinating meat longer than one hour, put it in a covered container and keep it in a refrigerator. Stir or turn strips as often as possible to make sure all surfaces absorb the flavors. Ground meat jerky benefits from longer marinating, but can be dried shortly after combining all the ingredients. The longer the marinating time, the more flavor is imparted. Note that it takes longer for a marinade to penetrate thicker, bigger pieces and that warmer marinades penetrate faster.

When removing strips from a marinade, put a bowl under a colander and let the marinade drain.

Before putting raw jerky in a dehydrator or smoker, first remove the drying trays, load them, and then return to begin the drying process. Strips need to lay flat, with no overlapping, in a single layer, leaving enough space between for dry air to circulate freely. On my 15-inch round dehydrator tray, I generally put ¾ to 1 pound of ¼-inch-thick strips. Depending on the airflow pattern in your drying environment, you may need to rotate the trays from the top to bottom every few hours during the drying process.

If you're drying something that gives off a strong odor, you can put your dehydrator outside, but note that wind can dramatically impact the drying.

How long it takes to dry meat into jerky will depend on the type of drying equipment, the quantity you are making, the number of trays, the moisture content, the size of the pieces, the humidity, and the drying temperature. In some instances, jerky can dry in a few hours or it may take days. With my 1,000-watt round dehydrator, eight trays of ¼-inch meat strips will dry in 6 to 8 hours and ground meat strips dry in 4 to 6 hours. Be aware, this is by no means a definitive time frame; fish and poultry can dry in as little as 2 hours.

To test when jerky is dry, first let it cool, because warm food always feels softer. Once dry, jerky should be flexible and bend without breaking, like a green twig. When squeezing a piece between your thumb and forefinger, you should not feel any moist spots. Jerky should not be crisp like a tortilla chip or so dry that it shatters. Crisp, brittle jerky means it was either dried too long or the temperature was too high. That said, when in doubt, it is still safer to over- than under-dry.

When dry, the moisture content of jerky will be reduced by as much as 90 percent. Most fresh meat, fish, and poultry contain 60 to 70 percent water—the medium that allows bacteria to grow. Dried, fresh meat reduces to between one half and one third of its original quantity, both in weight and volume. One pound of ground meat becomes about eight ounces of jerky and one pound of strips becomes half to a third pound.

A Cheap Trick

Our farrier was putting new shoes on our horses and raved about his sister's great jerky. After removing jerky from her dehydrator, she puts it in a sealable plastic bag along with half of a fresh habanero. She came up with this trick when she dried a batch of jerky too long and it got hard and she wanted to add a little moisture as well as enhance the flavor.

Once jerky is dry, it must be packaged and stored so it's not able to absorb moisture from air. If the jerky has not been sufficiently dried, mold can develop and, if found, the entire contents of the container must be discarded. However, do not confuse white ash on the surface of dried meats with mold; sometimes during the drying process, salt will rise to the surface, crystalize, and form a white film.

If jerky feels oily, wrap it in a paper towel to absorb any excess oil, then discard the toweling before packaging. This helps prevent rancidity and encourages longer shelf life.

Package dried jerky in airtight containers that have tight-fitting lids or use sealable plastic bags. Jerky can be kept at room temperatures for several weeks, but for long-term storage, it's best kept in a refrigerator or freezer.

To take along on a backpacking or camping trip, use self-sealing plastic bags and remember to label.

Although storage is a serious consideration, at our house it seems that jerky lasts only when I've located a good hiding place or when I make serious threats to anyone who has jerky breath. A lady in one of my classes offered her solution: "Wrap jerky in freezer paper and label it *liver.*"

PRETREATING

Marinades are either thick or thin sauces used to flavor raw meat, poultry, or fish. Marinades are combinations of various salts, sweeteners, and acids that act as tenderizers and also provide flavor along with various herbs, spices, fruits, and vegetables.

Brines are thin marinades with a high concentration of salt. Brines are also called wet cures and can be either hot or cold. A basic brine has one part salt and eight parts water (1 cup salt and 2 quarts water). The amount of salt used may depend on the size of pieces, with larger pieces requiring more. A warm brine will penetrate meat faster. During brining, place a lid or a plate on top of the container to weigh all pieces down

Old-time brines were heavily salted and produced almost inedible dried food. Most of the time, before being eaten, the dried meat and fish had to be soaked to eliminate the salt.

so they remain submerged. If foam appears under the lid, it should be skimmed off.

Dry cures are dry ingredients that are rubbed, pressed, or pounded directly onto the surface of meat, fish, or poultry. As flavors blend, dry cures draw water and blood out and oftentimes a brine-like liquid develops. A dry cure generally has two portions of salt, one portion of sugar, and various herbs and spices to add flavor. Usually 1 to 2 tablespoons of dry cure is used per pound of meat. Strips are laid in a single layer on a clean flat surface and the dry cure is liberally sprinkled on both sides. The strips are put in a covered glass or earthenware containers and refrigerated for 8 to 24 hours.

Cure Recipes from the Past

Venison Jerky Dry Cure

Our neighbor, Elton Redalen, a fifth-generation farmer, learned how to make venison jerky from his grandfather, who learned from his father, and so it went.

Elton mixed 2 cups of salt, ½ cup of brown sugar, and ¼ teaspoon of saltpeter (sodium nitrate) to use with 20 pounds of venison. He separated this mixture into thirds and spread one-third on ¼-inch venison strips. Then he put the strips in an earthenware crock and set in a cold environment. Every three days, he'd take the strips out of the crock and rub on another third of his dry cure. On the twelfth day, he removed the strips from the crock and hung them on hangers to dry in his attic.

Did You Know?

According to Minnesota deer hunter John Kvasnicka, each year about 8 million pounds of venison are processed in Minnesota alone. It's estimated that half is made into venison jerky or sausage. When commercial processors make jerky, they add pork, sodium nitrate, and various seasonings and the processing can cost at least $100 for a medium-sized deer.

A Dad Story

My dad was raised on a farm in the early 1900s. Every February, they butchered several 200-pound pigs. Grandma Bell made a brine that would float a raw egg, and for every 100 pounds of meat, she added 1 pound salt, ½ pound brown sugar, ⅓ cup of black pepper, and 3 ounces of saltpeter.

Hams were placed in the brine, which was covered with a tight-fitting lid that allowed no airflow. After the hams were brined at least 24 hours, they were removed and it was Dad's job to rub the dry cure all over the meat. The hams were checked every couple days to determine if more salt was needed. At the end of 30 days, the dry cure was washed off and the hams were smoked, then wrapped in muslin bags and hung from hooks in the granary.

The pig's revenge.

When pig-killing season was over, it was satisfying to think of the meat in the brine tub, the pots of lard, and the sausage and hams hanging from hooks. Dad told me a story about an unlucky old grandfather who insisted on taking a nap in his favorite armchair. One day he was resting in his armchair directly underneath a curing ham, it fell on his head, fractured his skull, and he died. The verdict? Homicide was the pig's revenge.

MARINADE INGREDIENTS

Because flavoring combinations are limitless, my best advice is to experiment. While developing the marinades in this book, my goal was not to mask or overpower the natural flavors of meat, fish, and poultry. Note that fish and poultry will absorb a marinade faster than red meat. And never reuse a marinade if blood has leached into it. When directions call for puréeing a marinade in a blender, remember, do not blend hot ingredients. Let them cool, then blend.

Jerky must contain some type of preservative and the easiest to add is salt.

Salt—sodium chloride (NaCl)—is the most common ingredient used in jerky making and serves as a very effective preservative. Salt helps us maintain our equilibrium of liquids and is as essential to human life as sun and water. We are in more danger of dehydration by not having enough salt than not having enough water.

As a rule of thumb, I add 1 teaspoon of salt per 1 pound of meat. Although 1 teaspoon is adequate, sometimes, like with Red Wine Jerky (see page 67), a second teaspoon can really perk up the taste. According to Dr. Maurer, 1 teaspoon of salt added to 1 pound of meat is more than just flavoring, because when dried, 1 teaspoon of salt will help inhibit the growth of microorganisms that cause spoilage, serve as a preservative, and lengthen storage life. Salt draws water and blood from muscle tissue and induces partial drying.

Choose good-quality, food-grade sodium, such as sea or kosher salt. Use a non-iodized salt if your intention is to heat a marinade or brine. Other salty options are soy, teriyaki, tamari, Bragg Liquid Aminos, and Worcestershire sauce.

Sodium nitrate, also called saltpeter, is a naturally occurring mineral substance considered a quick cure because as soon as it is put on meat, the color changes. Its pink color differentiates it from regular salt. When you put it on meat, it adds color, helps prevent spoilage, and retards bacterial growth. Sodium nitrite is powerful and potentially dangerous and can become toxic

> Because the tongue registers flavors first, sprinkle salt and other flavorings on top of the jerky right after you put it on the drying trays.

if too much enters the human body. The USDA recommends using only 6.1 grams of sodium nitrite to cure 100 pounds of meat. This is equal to roughly ½ teaspoon sodium nitrite, I highly recommend using an accurate kitchen scale when measuring sodium nitrite and other ingredients, for both safety and consistency reasons.

My marinades do not contain MSG (monosodium glutamate) or saltpeter; but some of the marinades I got from other people use commercial products that do contain various chemicals. You can check ingredient labels of unfamiliar products for such chemicals.

Sweeteners include white, brown, or cane sugar, maple syrup, honey, molasses, sorghum, and corn syrup. Small pieces of dried fruits, like cranberries, cherries, and mangoes add a touch of sweetness to a marinade, as do caramelized onions.

Oil enhances the texture of jerky and has a tenderizing effect. Olive, coconut, and sesame are my favorites, but consider using any flavored oil.

The problem with adding oil to a marinade is that it has the potential to bead up on the surface of the dried jerky. If this happens, just pat off the oil with paper toweling before packaging.

Drying Fat

Generally, fat will not dry; that said, I came across a seventeenth-century practice of preserving fat in the Faroe Islands, a group of eighteen islands in the North Atlantic near Iceland. They preserved mutton fat by cutting the tallow of sheep into pieces. It was allowed to rot, rendered, and the tallow chunks were cut into cubes and stored in earthen pits. The longer it was stored, the better it got, and when it got very old, it was reported to taste like cheese.

Smoking is a drying technique that adds flavor and has a preservative, antibacterial, and antioxidant effect. **Liquid smoke** is a popular marinade ingredient made by burning wood and then condensing the smoke and separating out the carcinogenic tars, resins, and soot. That means liquid smoke has less chemical residue than real smoke.

While researching liquid smoke, I found that one variety is made in my hometown, Manitowoc, Wisconsin, by the Red Arrow Company. The Red Arrow Company burns sawdust, a by-product of the wood industry, and then uses that to power its facilities.

In my opinion, most jerky recipes call for too much liquid smoke and the finished jerky tastes like smoke and little else. When using a smoker to dry jerky, it's unnecessary to add liquid smoke to your marinade.

Another option to consider is to put your almost dry jerky in a smoky environment for half an hour at the end of the drying process. This is a good idea because smoke adheres to a dry surface.

Corn Ash

Smoke has been used throughout time in many cultures to dry and flavor food. Buffalo Bird Woman of the Hidatsa tribe made corn ash by shelling corn and then burning the cobs. After they cooled, she discarded the surface ash and stored the cob ash in special containers. Corn ash was a key ingredient in her favorite dish—a mush made with various combinations of dried beans, squash, sunflower seeds, and corn.

FLAVORING AGENTS

A myriad of fresh, frozen, canned, cooked, and dried fruits and vegetables can be used to add flavor to marinades, brines, and cures. The creative potential is never ending. In addition to sautéed onions adding sweetness to a marinade, you can grate, mince, or finely chop raw onions. Choices range from raw radishes to dried coconut and from applesauce to chocolate. For a tomato flavor, use fresh, dried, or canned tomatoes, ketchup, tomato juice, paste, sauce, salsa, or V8 juice. Use fresh or dried garlic, horseradish, mustard, ginger, and peels of lemons, oranges, and limes. Various powders, such as dried cherry, celery, coconut, ginger, onion, celery, mango, chili, and especially wasabi powder can kick up the taste. Consider adding pieces of dried or fresh dill or sweet pickles, or beets and mushrooms, even sauerkraut to a ground jerky mixture. Dry cheese, like Romano or Parmesan, are great with ground meats. Liquids can range from vanilla to orange and pineapple juice to buttermilk or coconut milk, even espresso.

> Be careful not to add too large of pieces to flavor a ground meat jerky because they can block your jerky gun from firing.

Booze options include rum, vodka, triple sec, cheap scotch, whiskey, sherry, white wine, and beer. Then there is root beer and its concentrate as well as other soda pops.

Herb choices include basil, bay, cilantro, mint, oregano, parsley, rosemary, sage, savory, tarragon, fennel, and thyme. Herbs and spices can be added directly to a marinade or steeped like tea, strained, and then added.

Seed and **spice** choices include caraway, coriander, sesame, mustard, and celery seed as well as white, green, and pink peppercorns and juniper berries. Consider adding allspice, cardamom, cayenne, cloves, cumin, curry, nutmeg, paprika, star anise, cinnamon, cloves, or paprika.

Commercial cures and seasonings provide a fast and easy way to make jerky. Dehydrator manufacturers, specialty and spice shops, and the Internet are good hunting grounds for finding jerky mixes. Teriyaki, original, Cajun, mesquite, mountain, peppered, Hawaiian, Western, Jamaican jerk, jalapeño, and honey glaze seasonings are very popular. Mixes generally contain salt, a sweetener, and a preservative, along with various flavorings. When using store-bought mixes, follow their instructions. Two popular seasonings are Morton Tender Quick (a combination of salt, sodium nitrite, sodium nitrate, and sugar) and Accent, which contains monosodium glutamate (MSG). Other commercial sauces, like Tabasco, chili, taco, salsa, and barbecue offer easy and inexpensive flavoring options. Consider using dried mixes, like onion soup, Italian salad dressing, and taco seasonings. Generally a ⅛-ounce package works with 1 pound of strips or ground meat.

Tenderizers

Acids, like apple and rice vinegar, as well as alcohol, add flavor. They help meat reach its lowest water-holding capacity and help tenderize especially tough, gamey meats.

Know that alcohol evaporates and loses its alcoholic content during the drying process. Some marinades call for reducing alcohol to concentrate its flavor. To do this, use a high-sided pan to minimize the possibility of it catching on fire. If it does flame, it will die out as soon as the alcohol evaporates.

Smoking

After strips have been either dry-cured, brined, marinated, or cooked, they can be either **hot-**or **cold-smoked** in temperature-controlled smokehouses or drying ovens. **Hot** smoking temperatures generally range from 160 to 250 degrees. The higher temperatures melt fat and thereby reduce the potential of rancidity when storing jerky and can take as little as 2 hours. **Cold** smoking is slower with temperatures that range from 80 to 130 degrees. Once smoked, cold-smoked jerky must be kept refrigerated or frozen because the temperature did not get high enough to kill some pathogens.

A PROVEN JERKY THEORY

While doing post-doctoral work in Germany, Dr. Larry Borchert developed a theory based on his study of a type of pork that easily gave up its water.

He said, "This pork rapidly went down to an isoelectric point of pH 5.3, which meant it quickly reached its lowest water holding capacity." He speculated that if this type of pork became an ingredient in salami, it would dry faster. He made this reaction happen in other meats by adding organic acids, like vinegar and lemon juice, to help meat reach its lowest water-holding capacity.

Larry started hunting at the age of fourteen, so his profession and hobby worked well together. He experimented with ways to make jerky since the mid-1970s. His goal was to develop products for under-utilized red meat species, such as wild game, bison, ostrich, and emu.

After retiring as director of central research from Oscar Mayer Foods in 1996, Larry became an adjunct professor of meat science at the University of Wisconsin–Madison.

"Each ingredient plays an essential role," he explained. "Sodium nitrite is always included because without it meat loses its flavor. Soy sauce contributes salt and moves the pH in the right direction, but Worcestershire sauce is the key ingredient because of its drying effect."

His process started with trimming off all visible fat and connective tissue on either lean flank or round steak. He then froze the meat and brought it back to a semi-frozen state, cutting it into ⅛- to ¼-inch slices with the grain.

His recipe for 100 pounds of meat included 4 pounds salt, 4 ounces sodium nitrite (6.25 percent nitrite pre-mix), 8 ounces ground black pepper, 8 ounces garlic powder, 8 ounces onion powder, 5½ pounds soy sauce, and 6½ pounds of Worcestershire sauce.

He applied dry ingredients to semi-frozen meat slices and, as it thawed, the ingredients were absorbed. He left the treated meat for 24 hours at 40 degrees. Then he put the strips in another pan and dribbled soy sauce on each piece. The meat soaked up the soy sauce like a sponge. When all pieces were treated, it was cured again at 40 degrees for another 24 hours.

Finally, he added Worcestershire sauce, which helped the meat give up additional moisture. The next day, every

Note of Caution

Larry was able to make jerky at a low temperature because he added sodium nitrite. Without it, there would be bacterial risk.

bit of moisture had soaked up into the meat, leaving no brine. The strips were dried at temperature of 60 degrees or below. His jerky dried in 18 to 24 hours and came out flexible, with a mahogany color and a good natural flavor.

MARINADE OPTIONS

Do a Double-Dip a.k.a. a Two-Step

This technique is an antidote for when jerky becomes too crisp, gets too hard, has too little flavor or is just a failure. To fix it, soak the jerky in another marinade for a couple minutes and then re-dry it. Not only is this a good idea when the jerky you've dried doesn't have the right taste or texture, but it is also a good way to add more flavor. Not only has this rescued failed jerky, it has created some really fabulous new jerkies.

Another aspect of this technique is to half-dry your jerky, then remove it from the drying environment and marinade or apply another cure, then put it back in a drying environment and re-dry.

Sprinkle

Because the tongue detects flavor, sprinkle salt, pepper, or any seasoning on the top surface of a not yet completely dry jerky.

Brushing

This is similar to a double-dip. After meat strips have been placed in a drying environment and the surface moisture has dried off, use a brush and paint the top of the drying jerky with a thin coat of barbecue sauce, honey, or molasses.

Spraying

Instead of a brush, use an atomizer. Steep an herb (like with tea), add 1 teaspoon garlic powder and a drop of liquid smoke, put it in a squirt bottle, and spray the drying meat.

Vacuum It

With a home vacuum packer, put strips and marinade in a canning jar or vacuum sealer bag and create a vacuum seal. The force of the vacuum will push the marinade into the tissues and thoroughly penetrate all cells and shorten the marinating time.

JERKY CANDY

"Candy" is what Billy Hagberg called his beef, chicken, and turkey jerky. "People come in, stand in front of our meat counter, and we hand them a jerky sample," Billy said, flashing a warm, friendly smile. "They try a piece of this and a little of that and pretty soon they're acting like kids pondering which piece of candy they want next."

Billy makes jerky in his store, Hagberg's Country Market in Lake Elmo, Minnesota. This family market has provided meat, poultry, fish, and jerky to Minnesota and Wisconsin customers since 1938. He recalled, "My great-grandparents brought an old family sausage recipe from Sweden and that's how our business got started."

Billy uses a vacuum tumbler to marinate his raw top round beef, chicken, and turkey breast strips. He felt the resulting jerky is moister, tenderer, easier to chew, has a uniform texture, an outstanding aroma, and a rich color. "Getting that vacuum drum was the best decision we ever made," Billy boasted. "Before we got that vacuum unit, we had to soak meat strips in a marinade or brine for 24 to 48 hours, but with a vacuum drum, it takes about 20 minutes. We use fewer containers and need less floor and refrigerator space, less brine, and less salt."

His vacuum tumbler is a 20-gallon stainless steel cylinder drum that holds 35 to 50 pounds of meat strips. It has an opening on one side and a removable lid. Once the drum is filled and the lid is secured, a switch is flicked and the drum rotates. The vacuum pump draws air out of the chamber, creating a negative pressure. The meat pores open up and spread apart and the flavorings are forced deep into the tissues. After about 20 minutes, the process is complete.

A 50-pound capacity vacuum tumbler.

"You get three to four times higher concentration of flavor in comparison to long-term brining," Billy said. Salt leeches blood out of meat. Blood is a flavoring agent and, with long marinating or brining times, dried meat is less flavorful without it. With a vacuum tumbler, there is 100 percent absorption and zero waste, which means all the marinade goes inside the meat instead of pouring it down a drain. After the strips are tumbled, they "rest" overnight in the refrigerator before being spread on smoker trays. Because the strips are drier going into the smoker, the process is faster. He gets a more consistent product, the processing time is dramatically reduced, plus there's less risk of contamination, which is critical in meeting food-inspection standards.

Keep a Journal

Making jerky can become a very personal thing, so keep track of your successes (and failures) either in this book (there are note pages in the back) or a jerky journal. Note the fresh weight of meat, your flavoring choices, and include how long the jerky was marinated, brined, cured, and dried. Record the drying temperature. If smoked, the type of wood and how long it took. Jot down ideas on how to amend your recipes or techniques to improve your next batch. For example, if your jerky tastes too salty, the next time decrease the marinating time or reduce the amount of salt. If it's not salty enough, increase the salt and/or the marinating time.

CHAPTER 5
Making Strip Jerky

Whether drawn by curiosity or mysterious inner urges, the following jerkies should please your palate. Although making strip jerky can be as easy as sprinkling salt, pepper, and garlic on meat strips, imagine a sweet jerky, a coffee jerky, or a spicy tomato jerky.

Any kind of meat, poultry, or fish can be used in most of the recipes in this book, although some do recommend a particular type. Teriyaki jerky can be made with beef, venison, buffalo, poultry, or fish. Note that some marinades, like mole, can be thick, whereas teriyaki is watery thin. Don't let consistency concern you—thick or thin, they're all great.

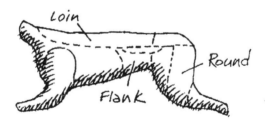

The process of making strip jerky is pretty easy: just cut, flavor, and dry. Select the leanest cuts possible, such as, flank, round, and loin. These cuts have less fat, gristle, membranes, and connective tissues. Choose boneless poultry breasts and skinned and filleted fish.

You can cut fat, gristle, membranes, and the connecting tissues off room temperature meat, but it's easier to cut strips when the meat is semi-frozen. Plus, freezing damages cells so the meat more readily gives up moisture. Electric slicers produce uniform-sized strips that dry in about the same amount of time.

By cutting across the grain, you get a jerky that's easier to chew. However, if you want more yank, cut with the grain. I cut ⅛- to ¼-inch-thick strips about 5 inches long. Note that the thinner the strips, the faster they absorb marinade and ultimately dry.

NATIVE JERKY

Larry Belitz and I share a love for the book *Buffalo Bird Woman's Garden*. This book tells about the lives of the Hidatsa people who lived in a village called Like-A-Fishhook on the Missouri River in North Dakota in the 1800s. It details how food was grown, cared for, harvested, preserved, and used.

Although Larry was not Native American, he was adopted into the Lakota tribe because of his passion for their ways. Over the years, he constructed thirty-three bison hide teepees like the Plains Indians; gave workshops on tanning, quill work, and flint knapping; and was involved in several documentaries, including as a technical advisor for the movie *Dances with Wolves*.

Larry was drawn to the native people's self-sufficient ways and how they lived with and off the land. "Everything revolved around the buffalo," he said. "It provided the first Americans with food, clothing, and a way of life. They shaped horns into utensils. Ribs became sled runners. Hides were used for ropes, shields, bullboats, parfleches, and teepees. Meat became jerky and pemmican." The Lakota call dried meat—whether it was deer, antelope, or buffalo—*bapa.*

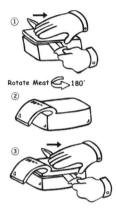

Rotate Meat 180°

Larry watched how they made jerky by using a knife beveled on one side. He learned how to turn a hunk of meat into one long continuous strip, like an accordion pleat. With one hand placed firmly on the meat to keep it flat, they cut with the grain. They stopped the knife ⅛ inch short of the other end so that the slab was not cut all the way through. The goal was to create a hinge that bends. The meat was turned 180 degrees and another cut was made, again stopping ⅛ inch from the end. This process was repeated until the last piece was ⅛ inch thick. When unfolded, it could be as long as 2 feet.

Larry said, "Sometimes the strong, dry South Dakota meat strips would dry in as little as two hours, rarely did it take more than a day."

MONTANA JERKY

I first met Glenda Ohs when she stopped by my booth at the Minnesota State Fair to talk about making elk jerky. Originally from northern Minnesota, Glenda moved to the Tobacco Root Mountain foothills in southwestern Montana in 1968. "You'd love it out here," she said enthusiastically. "Right outside my front window is Hollow Top Mountain. At almost 11,000 feet, its peak has snow year-round. Once I counted eighteen antelope, eighty-eight mule deer, and seven white-tailed deer. My little ranch is very productive," she said. On 1,070 acres, she raised alfalfa hay, barley, wheat, oats, canola as well as green pea seeds for the Jolly Green Giant. Over winter, she has pastured as many as 270 riding horses and, in spring, midwifed about 100 calving cows.

"Last fall, one of the men shot an elk and a deer. The important thing about big game is that the fat has to be completely trimmed off, because that's what carries the strong wild taste," she said.

Glenda Ohs cuts semi-frozen chunks of meat into pieces about ¼-inch-thick and 5 inches long. She puts a layer of strips in a crock, sprinkles with salt and pepper, adds a little liquid smoke, then adds another layer of strips, more salt, pepper, and smoke and tops it off with teriyaki sauce. She repeats this process until the crock is full. Then she covers it with a pie plate, puts a rock on top, and lets it sit in a cool room overnight. In the morning, she dries the strips in either a 160-degree dehydrator or a 180-degree oven.

TERIYAKI JERKY

Hands down, teriyaki has been the most popular jerky flavor. For a little kick, add a dash of hot pepper, a teaspoon of horseradish, and a pinch of ground ginger. Remember, the longer meat marinates, the more flavorful the jerky. "Give it at least 36 hours to marinate," Vince, my father-in-law, would say. He liked the flavor of natural smoke on his jerky, so he'd dry it three hours in his dehydrator and then finish it in his smoker. His recipe called for soy sauce, but we prefer teriyaki.

FOR 1 pound meat strips

½ cup teriyaki sauce • 1 tablespoon brown sugar • 1 teaspoon garlic, minced • 1 teaspoon salt • 1 teaspoon black pepper, coarsely ground • 1 teaspoon fresh ginger, finely grated • ½ teaspoon liquid smoke (optional)

FOR 5 pounds meat strips

3 cups teriyaki sauce • 2 heaping tablespoons brown sugar • 1 heaping tablespoon garlic, minced • 2 teaspoons salt • 1 tablespoon black pepper, coarsely ground • 2 teaspoons fresh ginger, finely grated • 1 teaspoon liquid smoke (optional)

With the exception of strips, mix all ingredients together. Allow the ingredients to rest at least 15 minutes for the flavors to blend. Taste and make personal adjustments. Add strips and marinate at least 1 hour. For a longer marinating time, place in the refrigerator in a covered container or in an airtight plastic bag. Use a colander to drain the marinade. Spread strips in a single layer and place in a drying environment.

If oil beads up during the drying process, pat it off with paper towels. The strips may need to be turned over during the drying process so both sides receive the benefit of dry, heated air.

Always let jerky cool before determining if it's done. When dry, jerky should bend without breaking, like a green twig. Store dry jerky in airtight containers.

JERKY JUDGE'S JERKY

One of Monte Carlson's pals shot an antelope and gave him enough to make jerky. "Antelope meat turns into great jerky," Monte said.

Even though I do not use prepackaged marinade mixes, I include this because it was one of Monte's favorites.

1 pound antelope strips

1 (1.25-ounce) package McCormick Meat Marinade Mix • ½ cup water • 1 tablespoon olive oil • 1 tablespoon orange peel, finely grated • 1 teaspoon liquid smoke • 1 teaspoon salt

Mix the packaged marinade and water according to the directions in a marinating container. Add oil, orange peel, liquid smoke, and salt. Allow the ingredients to rest at least 15 minutes for the flavors to blend. Taste and make personal adjustments. Add strips and marinate at least 1 hour. For a longer marinating time, place in the refrigerator in a covered container or in an airtight plastic bag. Use a colander to drain the marinade. Spread strips in a single layer and place in a drying environment.

SWEET JERKY

FOR 2 pounds meat strips

½ cup maple syrup • ½ cup brown sugar • ½ cup water • ½ cup soy sauce • ¼ cup sorghum • 2 teaspoons balsamic vinegar • 4 teaspoons kosher salt • 1 teaspoon light molasses • ½ teaspoon black pepper, freshly ground

FOR 10 pounds meat strips

1½ cup maple syrup • 1½ cup brown sugar • 1½ cup water • 1¼ cup soy sauce • ¾ cup sorghum • ½ cup balsamic vinegar • 3 tablespoons kosher salt • 3 teaspoons light molasses • 1½ teaspoons black pepper, freshly ground

With the exception of strips, mix all ingredients together. Allow the ingredients to rest at least 15 minutes for the flavors to blend. Taste and make personal adjustments. Add strips and marinate at least 1 hour. For a longer marinating time, place in the refrigerator in a covered container or in an airtight plastic bag. Use a colander to drain the marinade. Spread strips in a single layer and place in a drying environment.

ROSIE'S JUNIPER JERKY

When we were in New Mexico, we heard about this old way of making jerky. After cutting strips of meat, sprinkle with salt and then rub a mash of juniper berries on top. Bragg Liquid Aminos is a natural soy sauce alternative made from soy protein and does not contain preservatives, is gluten-free, and is non-GMO.

1 pound meat strips

½ cup Bragg Liquid Aminos • 3 tablespoons juniper berries, crushed • 2 tablespoons honey • 1 teaspoon black pepper, freshly ground

With the exception of strips, mix all ingredients together. Allow the ingredients to rest at least 15 minutes for the flavors to blend. Taste and make personal adjustments. Add strips and marinate at least 1 hour. For a longer marinating time, place in the refrigerator in a covered container or in an airtight plastic bag. Use a colander to drain the marinade. Spread strips in a single layer and place in a drying environment.

CAJUN JERKY

Leslea created this two-step process by coating marinated strips with a blackened cornmeal mixture. This was not only brilliant, but tasty, too. For more zip, add cayenne pepper, finely chopped jalapeño, green chiles, or habanero peppers.

STEP 1

1 pound meat strips • 1 cup buttermilk • 1 teaspoon Tabasco sauce • 1 teaspoon honey • 1 teaspoon coarse salt

STEP 2

3 tablespoons cornmeal • 1 tablespoon paprika • 1 tablespoon butter • ½ teaspoon sugar • ¼ teaspoon coarse salt • ¼ teaspoon garlic powder • ⅛ teaspoon cayenne • ⅛ teaspoon black pepper, freshly ground

Combine strips, buttermilk, Tabasco, honey, and salt in a marinating container and refrigerate overnight. Drain the marinated strips in a colander and set aside.

Heat a heavy, preferably cast-iron skillet to very hot. Mix the cornmeal and paprika and blacken in a hot skillet until at least half of the cornmeal looks burnt. Then add butter and blend. Remove from heat, put it in a bowl, and add sugar, salt, garlic powder, cayenne, and black pepper. Blackened mix can be hot, so allow it time to cool before adding the strips. Toss the strips of meat into the cornmeal mixture and try to coat all surfaces. Spread strips in a single layer and place in a drying environment.

COFFEE JERKY

The stronger the coffee, the more flavor. This marinade works really well with beef and gives off a great smell during the drying process.

1 pound meat strips

½ cup espresso • 2 tablespoons brown sugar • 2 tablespoons sautéed onions • 1 tablespoon garlic, roasted and mashed • 2 tablespoons balsamic vinegar • 1 teaspoon sea salt • ½ teaspoon black pepper, coarsely ground

With the exception of strips, mix all ingredients together. Allow the ingredients to rest at least 15 minutes for the flavors to blend. Taste and make personal adjustments. Add strips and marinate at least 1 hour. For a longer marinating time, place in the refrigerator in a covered container or in an airtight plastic bag. Use a colander to drain the marinade. Spread strips in a single layer and place in a drying environment.

CANDY JERKY

This is a simple two-step process. After the meat is flavored with maple syrup and soy sauce and has marinated for at least 24 hours, it's put in a drying environment for no more than 30 minutes to dry the surface moisture. Then it's removed, tossed into a bag with the seasonings, and dried.

1 pound meat strips

½ cup maple syrup • 3 tablespoons soy sauce • ½ cup white sugar • 1 tablespoon sea salt • 1 tablespoon garlic powder • 1 tablespoon onion powder • 1 tablespoon black pepper, freshly ground

Put meat, maple syrup, and soy sauce in a container and let marinate at least 24 hours. In a self-sealing gallon bag, add sugar, salt, garlic powder, onion powder, and pepper. The marinated strips need to be put in a drying environment to dry off the surface moisture. Then put the meat strips in the bag with the seasonings and make sure all surfaces are covered. Spread strips in a single layer and place in a drying environment.

MOLE JERKY

*M*_{ole}, a Nahuati word, pronounced, "MO-lay" is a chocolate sauce. However, a true mole is more than just a way to flavor meat with chocolate; it traditionally contains a triumvirate of dried chiles, such as mulato, ancho, and pasilla, plus seeds and spices.

2 pounds meat strips

3 ounces dried hot peppers • ½ cup water • 1 cup tomato juice, divided • ½ cup diced onion • 3 tablespoons sesame seeds • 2 tablespoons smooth peanut butter • 2 teaspoons salt • 1½ teaspoons ground cinnamon • 1 teaspoon ground coriander • ¼ teaspoon ground cloves • 3 ounces semisweet chocolate, chopped coarsely

Put dried peppers in a pan, cover with water, and slowly bring to a boil. Reduce heat and then simmer 30 minutes. Discard water. Add ½ cup tomato juice and purée. Strain to remove seeds and skin. Set aside. Combine all other ingredients, except chocolate, and mix well. Boil to reduce by a fourth. Add chocolate and stir until melted. Bring to a boil. Reduce again by a fourth. Cool and purée in a blender. Add pepper and purée. Allow the ingredients to rest at least 15 minutes for the flavors to blend. Taste and make personal adjustments. Add strips and marinate at least 1 hour. For a longer marinating time, place in the refrigerator in a covered container or in an airtight plastic bag. Use a colander to drain the marinade. Spread strips in a single layer and place in a drying environment.

Alcohol evaporates and loses its alcoholic content during the drying process. Some marinades call for reducing alcohol to concentrate its flavor. To do this, use a high-sided pan to minimize the possibility of it catching on fire. If it does flame, it will die out as soon as the alcohol evaporates.

RUM JERKY

This is the jerky that Gentleman Jim supplied to his sailing buddies and the one that got him into pursuing his own business.

2 pounds meat strips

¾ cup Myers's Rum • ¾ cup light brown sugar • ½ cup soy sauce • ⅓ cup Worcestershire sauce • ½ cup raw onions, finely minced • 2 tablespoons lime juice • 1 tablespoon fresh garlic, mashed • 1 teaspoon salt • ½ teaspoon chili powder

With the exception of strips, mix all ingredients together. Allow the ingredients to rest at least 15 minutes for the flavors to blend. Taste and make personal adjustments. Add strips and marinate at least 1 hour. For a longer marinating time, place in the refrigerator in a covered container or in an airtight plastic bag. Use a colander to drain the marinade. Spread strips in a single layer and place in a drying environment.

BLOODY MARY JERKY

Dip a strip of this jerky into a Bloody Mary instead of a stalk of celery or a dill pickle. You can also break this jerky into pieces and add a fistful to a spaghetti sauce.

2 pounds meat strips

¾ cup V8 juice • ½ cup vodka • ¼ cup Worcestershire sauce • 1 tablespoon honey • 1 tablespoon fresh horseradish, grated • 1 tablespoon lemon or lime juice • 1 teaspoon celery salt • 1 teaspoon hot sauce • ¼ teaspoon black pepper, freshly ground

With the exception of strips, mix all ingredients together. Allow the ingredients to rest at least 15 minutes for the flavors to blend. Taste and make personal adjustments. Add strips and marinate at least 1 hour. For a longer marinating time, place in the refrigerator in a covered container or in an airtight plastic bag. Use a colander to drain the marinade. Spread strips in a single layer and place in a drying environment.

JORDAN'S ROWDY JERKY

My niece, Diane, has a friend named Jordan who lives a very creative and rustic lifestyle in northern Wisconsin. In Jordan's world, jerky is not a luxury, but a staple.

My friend Larry Nelson, a retired Department of Natural Resources guy and experienced hunter, raved about how well this marinade worked with wild turkey, but did confess: "I added more scotch."

1 pound meat strips

¾ cup cheap scotch • ¼ cup brown sugar • 2 tablespoons soy sauce • 2 jalapeño peppers, chopped (with seeds) • 1 tablespoon olive oil • 1 teaspoon salt • ½ teaspoon liquid smoke • ¼ teaspoon black pepper, freshly ground

With the exception of strips, mix all ingredients together. Allow the ingredients to rest at least 15 minutes for the flavors to blend. Taste and make personal adjustments. Add strips and marinate at least 1 hour. For a longer marinating time, place in the refrigerator in a covered container or in an airtight plastic bag. Use a colander to drain the marinade. Spread strips in a single layer and place in a drying environment.

BOB'S BEST JERKY

Bob, an award-winning marksman, has spent a lot of time hunting and making jerky. Throughout the years, he has used this sweet, yet tangy marinade with deer, elk, and antelope.

1 pound meat strips

12 ounces canned root beer • ½ teaspoon root beer concentrate • ¼ teaspoon vanilla • 4 star anise • 1 bag peppermint tea • 1 tablespoon garlic, minced • 2 teaspoons kosher salt • ½ teaspoon black pepper, freshly ground • ¼ teaspoon liquid smoke

Put root beer and concentrate, vanilla, and star anise into a pan and heat to a boil. Remove from heat and drop in the tea bag, cover, and then steep for 10 minutes. Remove tea bag and anise and add the remaining ingredients except the meat strips. Taste and make personal adjustments. Add strips and marinate at least 1 hour. For a longer marinating time, place in the refrigerator in a covered container or in an airtight plastic bag. Use a colander to drain the marinade. Spread strips in a single layer and place in a drying environment.

DRY RUB CURRY JERKY

This is a good dry cure. Note that curry powders vary in smell, color, and taste.

1 pound meat strips

2 teaspoons kosher salt • 1 tablespoon brown sugar • 1 teaspoon curry powder
• ½ teaspoon ginger, ground • ½ teaspoon cumin • ¼ teaspoon garlic powder
• ¼ teaspoon black pepper, freshly ground

Combine all dry ingredients together, without strips. Use your hands to stir the ingredients together to make sure all the surfaces have received the benefit of the dry mixture. Cover and let sit at least 24 hours in the refrigerator or airtight plastic bag. If any liquid collects, drain, and then spread strips in a single layer and place in a drying environment.

BARBECUE JERKY

This sweet and sticky jerky is our granddaughter Alysse's most favorite. The word *barbecue* comes from a Spanish word *barbacoa*. It's the name of the greenwood lattice frame the Caribbean islanders used to hold strips of salted meat drying over a fire.

FOR 1 pound meat strips

¼ cup beer • 2 tablespoons cider vinegar • 2 tablespoons ketchup • 1 tablespoon olive oil • 1 cup raw onions, chopped • 2 tablespoons brown sugar • 2 tablespoons white sugar • 1 teaspoon Worcestershire sauce • 1 teaspoon soy sauce • 1 teaspoon ground ginger • 1 teaspoon kosher salt • ½ teaspoon garlic, minced • ½ teaspoon liquid smoke • ½ teaspoon Dijon mustard • ½ teaspoon celery seed • ¼ teaspoon black pepper, freshly ground • ¼ teaspoon cumin

FOR 10 pounds meat strips

2 cups beer • 1½ cups cider vinegar • 1 cup ketchup • ½ cup olive oil • 3 cups raw onions, chopped • 2 cups brown sugar • 1¼ cups white sugar • ½ cup Worcestershire sauce • ¼ cup soy sauce • 2 tablespoons ground ginger • ½ cup kosher salt • ¼ cup garlic, minced • 1 tablespoon liquid smoke • 1 tablespoon black pepper, freshly ground • 2 tablespoons Dijon mustard • 2 teaspoons celery seed • 2 teaspoons ground cumin

Rehydrate strips in beer, vinegar, and ketchup. Sauté onions in a fry pan with oil and then add a splash of water; cover, and cook until golden brown. Cool and then purée. Then add remaining ingredients with the exception of strips. Allow at least 15 minutes for flavors to blend. Add strips. Marinate at least 1 hour. For longer marinating time, place in the refrigerator in a covered container or in an airtight plastic bag. Remove from marinade and place in a drying environment.

FRUITY JERKY

Chef Mohammed El Assal from Madison, Wisconsin, developed the idea of a fruit jerky. Feel free to vary the dried and fresh herbs as well as the choice of fruit. This is a great jerky to use in the Parflech recipe on page 134.

2 pounds meat strips

½ cup dried cranberries • ¼ cup dried mango, cut in pieces • ½ cup pineapple juice • 2 tablespoons brown sugar • 2 tablespoons rice vinegar • 1 tablespoon balsamic vinegar • 1 tablespoon olive oil • 1 teaspoon salt • 1 teaspoon onion powder

Put cranberries and mango pieces in a blender with the pineapple juice and let rehydrate 10 minutes. Purée and add the remaining marinade ingredients, minus the meat strips, and purée until smooth. Taste and make personal adjustments. Pour over the meat strips and marinate at least 1 hour. For a longer marinating time, place in the refrigerator in a covered container or in an airtight plastic bag. Use a colander to drain the marinade. Spread strips in a single layer and place in a drying environment.

RED WINE JERKY

This is a great jerky to use in the Pasta con Carne Seca on page 148. For variety, add 1 teaspoon dried tomato powder and ½ teaspoon dried rosemary.

1 pound meat strips

3 cups red wine • 2 tablespoons white sugar • 2 teaspoons white vinegar • 2 teaspoons kosher salt

Cook the wine down to ¾ cup. Remove from heat and add meat, sugar, vinegar, and salt. Allow at least 15 minutes for flavors to blend. Marinate at least 1 hour. For longer marinating time, place in the refrigerator in a covered container or in an airtight plastic bag. Remove strips from marinade and place in a drying environment.

HERB JERKY

You can vary this marinade by adding fresh savory or thyme. Add 1 teaspoon green or red powdered chili pepper. For poultry, add 1 tablespoon lemon thyme. For fish, add 1 teaspoon fennel and chervil.

2 pounds meat strips

½ cup rice vinegar • 2 tablespoons brown sugar • 1 tablespoon olive oil • 1 tablespoon lemon juice • 1 tablespoon Worcestershire sauce • 1 teaspoon dried basil • 1 teaspoon dried oregano • 1 teaspoon dried cilantro • 1 teaspoon dried rosemary • 1 teaspoon sea salt • 1 teaspoon yellow mustard • ½ teaspoon celery powder • ½ teaspoon garlic powder • ¼ teaspoon black pepper, freshly ground

With the exception of strips, mix all ingredients together. Allow the ingredients to rest at least 15 minutes for the flavors to blend. Taste and make personal adjustments. Add strips and marinate at least 1 hour. For a longer marinating time, place in the refrigerator in a covered container or in an airtight plastic bag. Use a colander to drain the marinade. Spread strips in a single layer and place in a drying environment.

SWEET ADOBO JERKY

*H*ot is a relative word—for some, any pepper is hot, but others add a lot of habanero pepper and still claim the pepper not to be hot enough to make the jerky bite back. Depending on the amount of hot pepper you choose to use, you may want to have a drink within reach.

1 pound meat strips

2 cups buttermilk • ¼ cup kosher salt • ¼ cup honey • 1 teaspoon rice vinegar • 1 teaspoon soy sauce • 1 cup canned chipotle peppers, rough chopped

Mix all ingredients together with the exception of strips. Allow the ingredients at least 15 minutes for flavors to blend and the oil from peppers to distribute throughout the marinade before adding strips. Add strips and marinate at least 1 hour. For longer marinating time, place in the refrigerator in a covered container or in an airtight plastic bag. Remove from marinade and place in a drying environment.

JUDY'S HAM JERKY

Judy Lynch and her husband, Dan, have worked with horses all their lives. Judy's specialty is to arrange and conduct pack trips throughout North America. Several years ago, after leading a trip to the Bob Marshall Wilderness with eleven people and eighteen horses, Judy returned feeling defeated. "I didn't know if I'd ever be able to go on another pack trip unless somehow it got easier," she recalled. "Food preparation is the hardest part of a pack trip and my job is to provide delicious, hearty meals." Judy loves to cook and takes pride in serving good food. "I want everyone to sit around our campfire, smack their lips, and say, 'WOW! That was an incredible meal! How did you do that?'"

The trip to Montana haunted Judy until she came to one of my food-drying classes. She said her lightbulb turned on in class when she tasted the dried food samples.

The next summer, Judy returned to the Bob Marshall for a five-day pack trip with another large group, but this time she'd dehydrated all the main meals. As a result, all her kitchen and food supplies fit in one large duffel bag. "Drying food was the key," she said happily.

"I experienced less stress, my food budget was reduced, the horses packed lighter loads, and everyone loved the food, including my husband, who enjoys traditional home cooking. He said it was the best trail food he'd ever eaten."

"Ham jerky was the biggest hit. Everybody loved it," she said. "Riders always want something salty to snack on, and ham satisfied that desire—after all, bringing chips on a pack trip is not an easy task! It's good to have something salty, because it makes the riders drink more water, which most of the time, they don't do enough."

"I also liked that it was different," Judy added. "Most jerky is dried red meat, but the ham was a great treat, especially with dried pineapple. In addition, it rehydrated great and added zing and variety to my scalloped potatoes and split pea soup."

JUDY'S HAM JERKY

Throughout the years, people have asked about drying fresh pork and I tell them it's wiser to use ham. Vary the flavor with maple syrup or brown sugar. Ham slices can be used to make jerky, but I never use uncooked pork. Pink peppercorns are actually berries from a bush and not a member of the pepper family. Either cut slices ¼ inch thick, 1 inch wide, and several inches long, or to ultimately use for a cooking ingredient, cut into ½-inch squares.

1 pound ham strips

½ cup orange juice concentrate • ¾ cup honey • ¼ cup whiskey • 1 teaspoon prepared mustard • 1 teaspoon black pepper, ground coarse

Whisk orange juice concentrate and honey together and then add the remaining ingredients minus the strips. Let sit a few minutes before adding the ham slices and marinate at least 1 hour. For longer marinating time, place in the refrigerator in a covered container or in an airtight plastic bag. Remove from marinade, drain in a colander, and place in a drying environment. Sprinkle the tops of the ham strips with ground black pepper.

UNFORGETTABLE SPAM JERKY

Inside a brown envelope was a sheet of plain white paper that said, "Unforgettable SPAM Jerky." There was no name or return address.

This was too good to pass up, so with my curiosity sparked, I bought a can of SPAM precooked meat. My husband said the finished product reminded him of jerky he has purchased from gas stations.

1 (12-ounce) can SPAM

3 tablespoons soy sauce • 2 tablespoons water • 2 tablespoons brown sugar • 1 tablespoon Worcestershire sauce • ½ teaspoon fresh horseradish, grated • ¼ teaspoon chili powder • ¼ teaspoon liquid smoke • as much scotch bonnet sauce as you can handle

Cut SPAM into 12 slices and pile the slices one on top of each other. Then make two more cuts all the way through (the long way) to make a total of 36 pieces.

Put the remaining ingredients in a sealable plastic bag and swish around and then add the SPAM slices. Marinate 12 hours in the refrigerator. SPAM is a cooked product; therefore, it can be dried at any temperature. Do not overlap slices on drying trays. If any oil appears as a result of the drying process, pat dry with paper toweling before packaging. Dry until chewy, not crunchy.

JERK JERKY

Jerk spice originated in the Caribbean and allspice is the key ingredient. I've made jerk jerky with goat, venison, and beef. If you use goat, eliminate as much fat as possible because it can carry a strong flavor.

1 pound goat strips

1 teaspoon sea salt • ¼ cup lemon juice, freshly squeezed • 1 tablespoon cider vinegar • 1½ tablespoons ground allspice • 1 tablespoon olive oil • 1 tablespoon honey • 1 tablespoon garlic, chopped • 1 teaspoon scallions, minced • 1 teaspoon habanero pepper, finely diced • 1 teaspoon red chili powder • ½ teaspoon black pepper, freshly ground • ½ teaspoon nutmeg

Put strips in a bowl, sprinkle salt on top, and stir. Add lemon juice and vinegar. Mix together all remaining ingredients with the exception of marinating strips. Allow the ingredients at least 15 minutes for flavors to blend. Add strips. Marinate at least 1 hour. For longer marinating time, place in the refrigerator in a covered container or in an airtight plastic bag. Remove from marinade and place in a drying environment.

LEMONY LAMB JERKY

Lemon serves as a flavoring agent and the acid helps to create better texture. Historically, lamb was dried by rubbing sugar over a leg of mutton and then left for 24 hours. Over the course of a week, salt was rubbed on every other day. After that, it was brined 9 days, hung to dry another 3 days, and then finished by cold smoking.

1 pound lamb strips

½ cup lemon juice, freshly squeezed • ½ cup honey • 2 tablespoons fresh mint, finely chopped • 2 tablespoons olive oil • 1 teaspoon garlic, finely chopped • 1 teaspoon salt • ½ teaspoon black pepper, finely ground

Marinate strips in lemon juice at least 1 hour. Mix all remaining ingredients together and allow 15 minutes for the flavors to blend and then add strips. Marinate at least 1 hour. For longer marinating time, place in the refrigerator in a covered container or in an airtight plastic bag. Remove from marinade and place in a drying environment.

JERKED CHICKEN JERKY

Evan Clark sent an email asking me about taking jerky on a 4½-month-long backpacking trip on the Appalachian Trail with his soon-to-be wife. He wanted to send jerky ahead to food drop boxes and needed storage advice. The hike was to start at Mt. Katahdin, Maine, and end at Springer Mountain, Georgia.

I replied, "After your jerky has cooled and you've made sure it's thoroughly dry, either vacuum pack it or put it in heavy plastic bags and stash it in your freezer. Then just before your trip, take it out, check to make sure ice crystals have not formed inside the package, and send."

As we exchanged emails, Evan's story became more interesting. I learned that two years earlier, while walking the Appalachian Trail, he'd met the woman destined to become his wife. "She was heading north and I was heading south," he said. They exchanged business cards, corresponded, and this time had an Appalachian adventure together.

"I love the Appalachian Trail," Evan said. "I started backpacking to celebrate my fortieth birthday and carried sixty-three pounds on my back. It was torture. I had to make deals with myself. After I walked forty steps, then and only then could I stoop over and rest. I seldom took my backpack off because it was too painful to hoist on my back." With his jerky supply, his pack was just a little lighter.

EVAN'S JERKED CHICKEN JERKY

Evan started making his version of Jerked Chicken Jerky after returning from a stint as a Peace Corps volunteer in Jamaica—the island of wonderful food and exotic tastes. He loved the spicy/hot flavor of jerked chicken so much and wanted to be able to take it along on his backpacking trips, so he bought a dehydrator and experimented until he got his chicken jerky to taste just right.

1 pound boneless chicken breast, frozen

1 tablespoon olive oil • ½ cup lime juice, freshly squeezed • 2 teaspoons Walkerswood Traditional Jamaican Jerk Seasoning • 1 teaspoon salt

Cut partially frozen chicken into ¼-inch-thick slices, ½-inch wide, and no more than 5 inches long. Put oil, lime juice, jerk spice, and salt into a sealable plastic bag. Add strips and shake thoroughly so all the strips receive the benefit of the marinade. Marinate for at least 1 hour. For longer marinating time, place in the refrigerator in a covered container or in an airtight plastic bag. Remove from marinade and drain in a colander. Evan put the strips on a cookie sheet and baked them for 30 minutes, then let them cool before putting them in a drying environment.

CILANTRO TURKEY JERKY

Our neighbors, Andrea and Eric Miehlisch, raise organic turkeys and sometimes we're lucky and get some of their pristine meat. By lightly braising the marinated turkey strips, you get a tenderer jerky. Note that either raw or cooked poultry dries fast and needs to be checked each hour to determine if it is ready. Remember to let the strips cool a little before making your determination.

1 pound turkey strips

¾ cup buttermilk • ¼ cup dried cilantro • 2 tablespoons apple cider vinegar • 1 tablespoon brown sugar • 1 teaspoon sea salt • 1 teaspoon ground coriander seeds • 1 teaspoon garlic powder • 1 teaspoon onion powder • ½ teaspoon curry powder • ½ teaspoon black pepper, freshly ground

Combine all ingredients, with the exception of strips, whisk, and let sit for 15 minutes before adding strips. Marinate for 4 hours in the refrigerator in a covered container or in an airtight plastic bag. Drain in a colander. Put strips in a fry pan over low heat. As the color changes, turn each strip once and then cool before spreading strips in a single layer and placing in a drying environment.

A TROPHY HUNTER

Lee Hofer stated with both humor and conviction, "As much as three-quarters of the earth's surface is water and only one-quarter is land, the good Lord's intentions are clear—a man's time should be divided accordingly, three-quarters for hunting and fishing and one-quarter for work."

Lee has hunted all over the world and the evidence of his hunting prowess hangs on the walls at Lee's Meat & Sausage in Tea, South Dakota.

Lee's three computerized, stainless steel seven-feet-high and four-feet-square smokehouses can smoke one thousand pounds of meat at one time. He uses a blend of three different hardwoods, with hickory being dominant. Small wood pieces go in a stainless steel box on the side that automatically turns and drops the wood onto a hot plate, the smoke goes in the smokehouse, the dampers open, and for about 2½ hours, the meat is flooded with smoke.

His final comment was, "My life's goal was to combine my love of hunting and my work and I did it!"

WILD TURKEY JERKY

A wild 20-pound turkey has about 4 pounds of breast meat and generally we get another pound off the legs. We slice strips ¼ inch thick and as long as we can," Lee said.

1 pound wild turkey breast strips

½ cup honey • 4 tablespoons Morton Tender Quick • 4 teaspoons brown sugar • 2 teaspoons liquid smoke • 2 teaspoons black pepper • 2 teaspoons onion powder

Mix all the ingredients, with the exception of the strips, in a bowl. Add the turkey strips, mix thoroughly, and let sit overnight in the refrigerator. Spread strips in a single layer and place in a drying environment.

JERKING THE BLUE GOOSE

Bob Follmer loved to hunt, cook, and eat. When his doctor told him he had congestive heart failure and had to limit his salt intake, he was encouraged to stop eating jerky. Bob took control, bought a dehydrator, and started making his own jerky. "The salt-laden store stuff was history," Bob recalled. "They add salt because it's a cheap way to add flavor, and drinking establishments sell salty stuff to encourage their customers to drink."

After making his first batch of goose jerky, Bob took four pounds along on a trip to Grandville, North Dakota, with his hunting buddies. "During the eight-hour drive, they devoured it all," he said. "Since that trip, they expect jerky every time we get together," he chuckled. "We hunt blue and snow geese. They're greasier birds than honkers and I've tried every which way to eat them and then, out of necessity, I started making jerky."

Bob handed me a sample of his jerky and it was sweet and tart.

"My goose marinade can work with any meat," he said. "I've used it for venison, turkey, beef, and anything I can get my hands on. It has more flavor than any other recipe I've tried." Bob methodically kept a journal of his jerky-making experiments since 1979.

After skinning the bird, he uses the breast and thigh for jerky, leaving the bony legs behind. "You've got to get rid of all the fat or your jerky will taste rancid," he cautioned. He cuts the raw, purplish goose meat in strips ¼ inch thick and 1 inch wide.

Although Bob has made goose jerky in his electric smoker and in the oven, he prefers using a dehydrator because it makes sampling easier. "The smell of goose jerky drying drives me nuts," he confessed. "I can't wait until it's ready and keep opening up the lid to test it."

GOOSE JERKY

Bob said, "When I make this jerky for my wife, she doesn't like it hot, so I eliminate the Tabasco sauce and pepper. However, my buddies like it hot, so I kick it up a notch by adding three tablespoons of habanero pepper powder."

When I asked about how he stored his jerky, he grinned. "My jerky never makes it that far. If my family doesn't get it, the neighbors do."

4 pounds goose strips

1 can beer • ½ cup cheap red cooking wine • ½ cup light soy sauce • ¼ cup Worcestershire sauce • ¼ cup Kikkoman teriyaki sauce • ¼ cup lemon juice • 1 tablespoon liquid smoke • 1 tablespoon onion powder • 1 tablespoon garlic powder • 1 tablespoon Accent seasoning • 1 tablespoon Tabasco sauce • 1 tablespoon Caribbean jerk seasoning • 1 teaspoon black pepper

Put all the marinade ingredients in a large plastic bowl, blend, then add the strips. Cover the bowl and put it in the refrigerator. Turn the meat every 12 hours, so everything is soaked well. Marinate 48 to 96 hours. Bob dried the strips in a dehydrator at 155 degrees. "After about 10 hours, my jerky is soft, easy to chew, and good tasting, which is how I like it," he said. "I leave some in 14 hours for my sons because they like it dried rock hard."

TROUT JERKY

While testing these recipes, my husband, Joe, landed an 18-inch brown trout and he hesitantly sacrificed it to the jerky cause. Joe never liked fish jerky, but after a few hours of drying, I checked to see how the trout was doing and every single piece was gone. He had eaten it all—not one piece made it into a storage container!

1 pound cleaned trout strips

¼ cup soy sauce • 2 teaspoons maple syrup • 1 tablespoon lemon juice • 1 teaspoon salt • 1 teaspoon sesame oil • 1 teaspoon garlic, minced • ½ teaspoon black pepper, freshly ground

Mix together all ingredients, with the exception of the trout strips. Allow the ingredients at least 15 minutes for flavors to blend. Add strips and marinate at least 1 hour. For longer marinating time, place in the refrigerator in a covered container or in an airtight plastic bag. Remove from marinade and place in a drying environment.

TAKU FISHERIES

Taku is the Tlingit Indian name for the bitter cold wind that blows through the Taku River Valley in Southeastern Alaska.

In 1978, Sandro Lane went to work in Alaska as a marine biologist, but it didn't take long for him to decide he wasn't cut out to be a government worker. He'd fallen in love with Juneau, however, and didn't want to leave. "I'd gotten pretty good at catching fish and then I got even better at smoking them," he chuckled. "For years, I'd lived in Italy and learned how to cold-smoke lox and the basic process of curing meat and making salami. So I started messing around and put what I'd learned together and came up with our salmon jerky."

In 1984, after converting his garage into a food processing plant, Sandro perfected his cold-smoking technique. He received a US Small Business Administration loan and Taku Smokeries moved into a larger building in downtown Juneau. By 1992, Taku Smokeries occupied more than 3 acres with more than 40,000 square feet of warehouse space. In 2000, Taku Smokeries and Taku Fisheries annually processed over 6 million pounds of fish and continues to do about $20 million worth of business in both domestic and foreign markets.

Making salmon jerky starts with a de-headed, gutted, and filleted fish that's been skinned and pin-boned and then marinated in a brine. "Our brine time is measured in hours, not days—usually 12 and done in a refrigerator," Sandro stated. After the salmon is removed from the brine, it's quickly frozen and cut lengthwise with a band saw, creating ¼-inch-wide strips that are as long as possible. The strips are salted and hung on smokehouse racks, where light alder wood smoke is applied for 12 to 16 hours. "It takes 1,000 pounds of fresh fish to make 150 pounds of deep red, paper-thin, original or peppered salmon jerky."

The only thing Sandro didn't tell about his salmon jerky business was how much salt he put in his brine. "I'll give you a clue," he said. "Take a fresh, unpeeled potato, stick a 10-penny nail in it, drop the potato in a gallon of water, and add salt until the potato floats. Always keep track of the amount of salt you've added. Then note if your finished jerky tastes too salty or not salty enough. Then with the next batch, add more or less and either shorten or lengthen the brining time."

"All the racking and packaging is done by hand," Sandro said. "Our salmon is different from other salmon jerkies that grind fish, extrude it through a nozzle, dry on flat sheets, cut in small pieces, and package.

"Our salmon is good for you," Sandro said brightly. "It does not

Sandro Lane holding soon-to-be salmon jerky.

contain any preservatives or binders and no colors or flavors are added. Plus it has a high concentration of omega-3 oil." According to the Alaskan Seafood website, omega-3 oils produce a series of eicosanoids that have been shown to decrease the risks of heart disease, can reduce inflammation, and may prevent some types of cancer.

Sandro feels that one of his business's biggest accomplishments was that, in the early days of his business, the Japanese were his best customers. "They eat a lot of fish and have the most knowledge and the highest standards," Sandro explained with pride.

In my opinion, Taku Smokeries deserves a gold star for environmental awareness. They ship their products in insulated Styrofoam boxes and, to keep the Styrofoam out of landfills, they ask their customers to send the box back. Then the customer gets a $15 credit on their next order. "Our salmon comes from the unspoiled waters of Southeast Alaska and our business is dependent on a clean environment," Sandro said. "We believe this policy just makes good sense."

SWEET SOY SALMON JERKY

1 pound salmon strips

½ cup soy sauce • ¼ cup pineapple juice • 2 tablespoons brown sugar • 1 tablespoon molasses • 1 teaspoon liquid smoke

Mix together all ingredients, with the exception of the salmon strips. Allow the ingredients at least 15 minutes for flavors to blend. Add strips and marinate at least 1 hour. For longer marinating time, place in the refrigerator in a covered container or in an airtight plastic bag. Remove from marinade and place in a drying environment.

HONEYED SALMON JERKY

This is the perfect jerky to use to make the Salmon Jerky Loafettes on page 155.

1 pound salmon strips

¼ cup honey • ¼ cup rum • 1 tablespoon lemon juice • 1 teaspoon peppercorns, crushed • 1 teaspoon salt

Mix together all ingredients, with the exception of the salmon strips. Allow the ingredients at least 15 minutes for flavors to blend. Add strips and marinate at least 1 hour. For longer marinating time, place in the refrigerator in a covered container or in an airtight plastic bag. Remove from marinade and place in a drying environment.

SEEDY FISH JERKY

After receiving advice from some serious smelt fishermen, I learned to cut off the heads and tails and make a slit down the smelt's belly. Next, I rinse it with clean water and use my thumbs to pinch the spine and pull it out. Again I rinsed the smelt before beginning the marinating process.

1 pound smelt strips

¼ cup brown sugar • ¼ cup soy sauce • 1 teaspoon garlic, minced • 1 teaspoon salt • ½ teaspoon fresh ginger, grated • ¼ cup white sesame seeds

Mix together all ingredients, with the exception of the smelt strips and the sesame seeds, and allow the ingredients at least 15 minutes for flavors to blend. Add strips and marinate at least 1 hour. For longer marinating time, place in the refrigerator in a covered container or in an airtight plastic bag. Remove from marinade and place in a drying environment. Sprinkle sesame seeds on top of the smelt.

TERIYAKI TUNA JERKY

Tuna is the perfect medium for absorbing flavor. I think it would be impossible to mess up a batch of tuna jerky.

1 pound tuna strips

⅓ cup teriyaki sauce • 2 tablespoons brown sugar • 1 tablespoon olive oil • 1 tablespoon lime juice • 1 teaspoon fresh ginger, grated • 1 teaspoon salt • ½ teaspoon garlic, minced • ¼ teaspoon dried tarragon

Mix together all ingredients, with the exception of the tuna strips. Allow the ingredients at least 15 minutes for flavors to blend. Add strips and marinate at least 1 hour. For longer marinating time, place in the refrigerator in a covered container or in an airtight plastic bag. Remove from marinade and drain in a colander. Spread strips in a single layer and place in a drying environment.

MIKE'S WILD CATFISH JERKY

Fishing is in Mike Valley's blood. As a boy, he learned how to fish the Mississippi River with his father, just like all the men in his family had done since the mid-1800s. Mike was fourteen when he launched his own boat and ran gill nets for buffalo and sheepshead carp.

Every morning, before sunrise, from April through October, Mike, a strong, muscled man, steps into his 24-foot aluminum boat, starts his 230-horse Johnson engine, and does what he loves most—he gets out on the Mississippi River.

While visiting his shop, which overlooks the great Mississippi in Prairie du Chien, Wisconsin, Mike said, with a boyish Huck Finn glint in his eye, "I love that river. Everything else is work. Time on the river is my payoff. There have been times the water was so high that when I raised my nets, I had a thousand pounds of fish."

Mike shared his fascination with the wild catfish. "They're spooky," he said. "You can be looking at your fish finder, thinking there's a solid object right underneath you. But it isn't. It's a hundred catfish tightly bound in their underwater community. If I'd drop something, they'd spook and explode in as many different directions as fish in the cluster." He looked around. "In my opinion, the mud-cat is a better-tasting fish than the channel-cat. The worse something smells, the more likely a channel-cat will bite on it," he chuckled. "That should give you an indication of what it eats. I use the mud-catfish for jerky because it dines only on live bait. Some people call the mud-cat a flathead. They are nest builders and the parents look out for the young until they are able to disperse. Their young go to school, like our kids," he laughed. "When they get a little older and school gets out, they go their own way. The first year, they're about six inches in length. As adults they can reach over 20 inches and weigh 30 pounds or more. There are fishing claims of 50-pound catfish being caught between Clinton, Iowa, and Prairie du Chien, Wisconsin!"

Mike began working on his catfish jerky in the early 1980s. "It took years to get it right," he said. "The mud-cat has less oil than the channel-cat and doesn't burn as easily during the hot smoke drying process." His eyes darted toward the Mississippi. "I like the wild catfish."

Mike and his wife, Lisa, fillet the fish, make their own brine, dry the fish in their smokehouse, and sell jerky in their shop.

The process begins after about 500 pounds of fresh fish has been de-headed and gutted, and then Mike fillets the belly pads. "This generally takes about six hours. Then the most important thing is to spray the fish with cold water, let them drain, and not wash again," Mike instructed.

He lifted the top off a blue 30-gallon plastic tub, reached in, and held up a handful of fish strips he'd prepared 24 hours earlier. "I cut fillets ¼ inch thick, ½ inch wide, and 5 or 6 inches long. We use a hot brine cure." Then, looking a bit stern, he announced, "And I'm keeping my brine recipe a secret. You can use any jerky brine, but be careful when adding salt. Too much salt can ruin your jerky." He lets his brine boil 1 minute, then simmers it for 10 minutes, and then lets it cool before adding the fish strips.

Mike picked up the blue container and walked from the processing room to a screened-in porch behind his shop, which

Mike Valley placing marinated catfish on his smoker.

smelled intensely of smoke and fish. A huge blackened metal box dominated the room. It stood about seven feet high and was about eight feet long and four feet deep and had six enormous drawer-like trays. Mike pulled out a tray, grabbed a steel brush, and scraped the blackened steel. His rough, weathered hands revealed a life of hard work. With the trays clean, he pulled open the bottom tray and spread out a handful of marinated fish strips. After spending two hours carefully positioning each fish strip flat on all six trays, he almost whimsically sprinkled a mixture of finely ground pepper, dried sweet basil, and dried oregano over the strips. He went behind the smoker, picked up a large cup, and scooped two pounds of oak and hickory wood chips into a paper bag. He squatted down, opened the fire door, stuffed the bag in, laid two sticks on top, and struck a match. The fire caught and he shut the door. "I like a mixture of chips." The teacher in him reappeared: "Never use pine or cedar because they make jerky turn black."

He put one hand on his back and struggled to stand. "I don't use wood that's been sprayed. It's got to be clean, without dirt and mold and not wormy. I like adding a little green hickory because it produces good smoke," he said, adding more wood. "We burn about six truckloads of split hickory a year."

He checked the smokehouse thermometer. "It has to hit 160 degrees and stay there at least 30 minutes, so I need to keep my eye on it. A whole batch can burn in just a few minutes." He stepped back.

"It's done after about 4 hours and my fish jerky has a beautiful golden color."

Lisa, a friendly and attractive brunette, handed me a sample of their wild catfish jerky. "The Wisconsin inspector said our smoke shop was the cleanest in the state."

"It smells stronger than it tastes," I said.

Mike smiled. "The quality standards we insist upon must be working because we keep running out of our catfish jerky."

They also make various flavors of fish jerky as well as snapping turtle, chicken, pork, salmon, bison, and alligator.

MIKE'S WILD CATFISH JERKY

Cut catfish strips ½ by ¾ inches and 5 inches long. Catfish is oily, and once it's dry it may need to have any excess oil patted off before it's packaged.

3 pounds catfish strips

4 cups water • ½ cup soy sauce • ½ cup sesame teriyaki sauce • ½ cup Mr. Yoshida's sauce • ⅓ cup brown sugar • 3 tablespoons salt • 1 tablespoon dried sweet basil • 1 tablespoon rosemary garlic • 1 tablespoon lemon pepper • 1 tablespoon black pepper, finely ground • ½ tablespoon powdered garlic

Put catfish in a bowl with all the other ingredients. Thoroughly mix and let marinate overnight or for at least 6 to 8 hours in the refrigerator in a covered container or in an airtight plastic bag. Remove from marinade and place in a smoker for 3 to 4 hours, or until dried.

SPICY HALIBUT JERKY

My memory of halibut goes back to when I was a kid. We lived in a Catholic community and on Friday meat was off limits. I sure would have liked to have this jerky instead of some of the bland fish we had available.

1 pound halibut strips

1 cup onion, thinly sliced • 1 tablespoon olive oil • ½ cup orange juice concentrate • 1 tablespoon jalapeño pepper, finely minced • 1 tablespoon soy sauce • 1 tablespoon garlic, minced • 1 tablespoon honey • 1 teaspoon Tabasco sauce • 1 teaspoon salt • 1 teaspoon fresh ginger, grated • ¼ teaspoon black pepper, freshly ground

Sauté onions in olive oil and mix with all the other ingredients, with the exception of the halibut strips. Allow the ingredients at least 15 minutes for flavors to blend. Add strips and marinate at least 1 hour. For longer marinating time, place in the refrigerator in a covered container or in an airtight plastic bag. Remove from marinade and place in a drying environment.

SOLEFUL JERKY

After the previous "holy" jerky, what could be better than Soleful Jerky? This mild, yet flavorful jerky can vary by using other juices in the marinade.

1 pound sole strips

¼ cup lemon juice, freshly squeezed • 1 teaspoon Dijon mustard • 1 teaspoon salt • 1 teaspoon dried dill, crushed • 1 teaspoon garlic, minced • 1 teaspoon white sugar • ¼ teaspoon black pepper, freshly ground

Mix together all ingredients, with the exception of the sole strips. Allow the ingredients at least 15 minutes for flavors to blend. Add strips and marinate at least 1 hour. For longer marinating time, place in the refrigerator in a covered container or in an airtight plastic bag. Remove from marinade and place in a drying environment.

Making Ground Meat Jerky

Making jerky out of ground meat has become very popular. It is easier to make than using strips, takes less time to prepare than the cutting and handling of strips, it tastes great, and it's less expensive. It dries faster, is easier to chew than strip jerky, and the ground meat absorbs all the marinade. Plus, with ground meats, you can mix various types of meat together— like half turkey and half beef, or half ground venison (it's often too lean) and half (a fattier) ground beef.

When using ground meat, you can add an almost limitless variety of flavorings to the mixture. Consider adding small pieces of dried mango, papaya, cranberries, or cherries, or chunks of fresh or dried dill or sweet pickles. How about dressing up a meat mixture with cherry, celery, or wasabi powder? You can add cheese, like dehydrated blue or Romano. To add a tomato flavor, choose fresh, canned, dried, or powdered tomatoes, or salsa and ketchup. Don't forget both fresh and dried mushrooms.

With all that said, making jerky from ground meats can be challenging. The goal is to create a jerky that holds together, is tender, and is not too dry or crisp. One solution to getting ground meat to hold together is adding 1 teaspoon of salt to the raw meat and then using a potato masher to force the salt into it. Another solution is to add foods that serve as binders, like instant mashed potatoes or either raw or cooked oatmeal. Oil also serves as a binder, helps tenderize meat, improves texture, and adds flavor.

However, being able to predetermine the fat content of meats can be difficult. For example, wild or grass-fed meat does not contain enough fat to act as a binder and store-bought can have too much. In this case, you can easily blend two different types of meat together. I prefer ground meat that's about 90 percent lean, but when a recipe calls for a lot of dry ingredients, I use 85 percent lean. If there's too much oil during the drying process, it will rise to the surface of the jerky. The response is to pat the jerky with paper towels, soak up any excess oil, and then put it in a storage container.

Another option is to mix the ground meat together, do a sample test, and dry with just a small amount. See what you get and, if it's too dry or crisp, add more oil.

With ground meat jerky, you need to pay attention to the amount of liquid in a marinade because all of it needs to be absorbed.

Before being able to smoke a ground meat jerky, the strips will need to be dried long enough to maintain their shape.

Although any ground meat can be used with many of these recipes, some suggest one specific type of meat, poultry, or fish.

When using frozen meat, take care how you thaw it. I believe naturally thawed meat helps foster a better texture in dried jerky than when it has been thawed in a microwave. This is especially true with any ground meat.

A Pain in the Tuchus

Every August, I packed my portable display booth into my van along with 20 pounds of jerky, several gallon bags of dried apples and bananas, and enough applesauce fruit rollup to satisfy every hungry kid that walked past me in the Agriculture Horticulture Building at the Minnesota State Fair. I knew that tasting dried foods, especially jerky, was the quickest way to engage a fair-goer in a discussion about drying food. Over 12 challenging, 14-hour days each year, I answered thousands and thousands of food drying questions—most of which had to do with making jerky.

One day while demonstrating my jerky gun, I heard giggles, then a couple of guffaws from people standing in front of me.

"Why are you laughing?" I asked, holding my loaded jerky gun.

A young athletic woman responded, "Making jerky at our house is a real pain in the tuchus. We like ground beef jerky and we shape the seasoned ground meat into a ball about the size of a softball. We put a sheet of waxed paper on top of a cutting board, plunk the meat down, put another piece of waxed paper on top, and another cutting board on top of that." She squeezed her partner's arm. "Then he plunks his posterior down and flattens. That's why we call jerky-making a pain in the tuchus." They looked at each other, smiled, got out their charge card, and bought a jerky gun, knowing it would save them a lot of muss and fuss. "But it won't be as much fun," the woman said and then disappeared into the sea of fair-goers.

TAKE AIM WITH A JERKY GUN

A Nesco jerky gun with several different nozzle tips.

Flavored ground meat can be shaped into ⅛- to ¼-inch-thick strips or round sticks with clever gadgets called *jerky guns* or *jerky shooters*. They look like caulking guns or cake decorators. The barrel is filled with a ground meat mixture and, when the trigger is pulled back, it extrudes meat into a uniform shapes and sizes depending on which nozzle tip is used. Generally, 1 pound of ground meat becomes 10 to 12 strips that measure ¾ inch wide and 5 to 6 inches long.

Jerky gun strips on a drying tray.

After extruding the jerky onto the drying surface, use a spoon to rub over the strips so they are smooth and do not have lumps, bumps, or breaks.

IF GUNLESS

If you don't have a gadget to form the meat mixture, you can use your hands. Meat is less sticky and easier to handle when it is cold. It also helps to wet your hands.

Shape a heaping tablespoon of ground meat mixture into a ball. Put it on top of a piece of plastic wrap or waxed paper and cover with another piece. With a rolling pin, flatten the ball into ¼-inch-thick rounds about 2 inches in diameter. Uniform thickness will help jerky dry in about the same amount of time. When checking for dryness, make sure the center of the patty has been sufficiently dried.

ANOTHER GUNLESS OPTION

Most food dehydrators have plastic liner sheets that fit inside a tray and are called either Fruit Leather or Roll-up sheets.

Spray or spoon a little oil onto one of these plastic liner sheets. Then spoon the ground meat mixture on top and, with either your hands, a spatula, or a wooden spoon, evenly flatten the meat to no more than ¼ inch thick. Place this meat-filled sheet in a dehydrator and dry long enough that you can use a pizza cutter or a serrated knife to make indentations or cut lines about 1 inch apart in the drying meat. Return to the dehydrator and dry until the meat strips can be broken at the cut lines. Take the strips off of the plastic liner sheet and place on a dehydrator tray without the sheet. This allows more air movement throughout the drying process.

FUN JERKY—A PLAYFUL ALTERNATIVE

I learned another technique while packing up after a doing a food-drying presentation for a local Scout troop. A dad offered to help schlep my stuff to my van and on the way, he said, "I'd like to share an idea with you." Then he told me about how his whole family participated in making jerky. "We homeschooled our kids and like to approach life creatively and we use a Play-Doh Fun Factory to shape ground meat jerky. It's fun to make jerky into various shapes. Try it!" he encouraged.

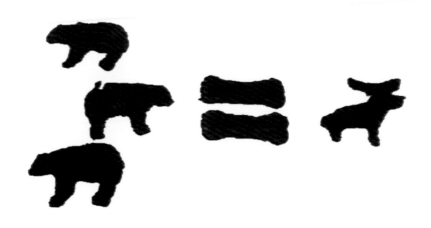

Fun animal shapes made out of ground meat jerky.

You can do the same thing without any special tools or toys. This is not only fun, but it's also a good way to get kids involved in making jerky.

Spread a sheet of waxed paper on your counter top. Spoon some flavored meat mixture on it and put another sheet of waxed paper on top of that. Use a rolling pin to flatten the mixture to about ¼ inch thick. Take off the top sheet of waxed paper and press animal-shaped cookie cutters firmly down to make impressions in the mixture. For example, use a deer shape for venison and a cow for beef.

Carefully lay the animal shape on a solid plastic sheet. Dry until it becomes firm and then take it off and place it on a drying tray so air can more easily get to it. When checking for doneness, make sure the center is completely dry.

PAN JERKY

Line a loaf pan with aluminum foil or cellophane wrap. Press the meat mixture into the pan and put it in the freezer until it is frozen enough to hold together. Remove it from the pan and slice it into ¼-inch strips, then dry.

TERIYAKI JERKY

My father-in-law, Vince Deden, used soy sauce and eliminated the liquid smoke to modify this recipe. Then, just before the jerky was dry, he put it in a smoker for about 1 hour. Taste-testers agreed that spending a Sunday afternoon watching a sporting event with a piece of jerky in one hand and a cold beverage in another was great fun.

FOR 1 pound ground meat

1 teaspoon salt • ⅓ cup teriyaki sauce • 1 teaspoon olive oil • 1 teaspoon brown sugar • 1 teaspoon garlic, minced • ½ teaspoon black pepper, coarsely ground • ½ teaspoon fresh ginger, finely grated • ¼ teaspoon liquid smoke

FOR 5 pounds ground meat

1 tablespoon salt • 1½ cups teriyaki sauce • 2 tablespoons olive oil • 2 tablespoons brown sugar • 1 tablespoon garlic, minced • 1 tablespoon black pepper, coarsely ground • 1 tablespoon fresh ginger, freshly ground • 2 teaspoons liquid smoke

Put meat and salt in a bowl and use a potato masher to force the salt into the meat. Combine all the other ingredients in a bowl and then wait a few minutes for the flavors to blend. Add the salted ground meat and thoroughly mix. Put in a covered container or a self-sealing plastic bag. If marinating longer than 1 hour, place in the refrigerator. Because cold meat is harder to put through a jerky gun, let the mixture warm up for a few minutes before forming into strips and putting in a drying environment.

AN ORIGINAL TWIST

Original is a very popular commercial jerky and its ingredients are well-guarded secrets. A label on a popular Original seasoning packet listed dextrose, salt, natural spices, hickory smoked flavor, onion powder, garlic powder, MSG, hydrolyzed vegetable protein, and imitation maple flavor. Its cure packet contained salt and sodium nitrate.

With my version, my family felt that the peppercorns were the needed ingredients. For variety, add 1 tablespoon tomato sauce, 1 teaspoon minced garlic, and ½ teaspoon white pepper.

1 pound ground meat

1 teaspoon salt • ¼ cup soy sauce • 2 tablespoons brown sugar • 2 tablespoons white sugar • 1 tablespoon pepper, finely ground • 1 teaspoon onion powder • 1 teaspoon garlic powder • ½ teaspoon liquid smoke • ½ teaspoon pink peppercorns, finely ground • ¼ teaspoon green peppercorns, freshly ground • ¼ teaspoon white peppercorns, freshly ground

Put meat and salt in a bowl and use a potato masher to force the salt into the meat. Combine all the other ingredients in a bowl and then wait a few minutes for the flavors to blend. Add the salted ground meat and thoroughly mix. Put in a covered container or a self-sealing plastic bag. If marinating longer than 1 hour, place in the refrigerator. Because cold meat is harder to put through a jerky gun, let the mixture warm up for a few minutes before forming into strips and putting in a drying environment.

THREE SISTERS JERKY

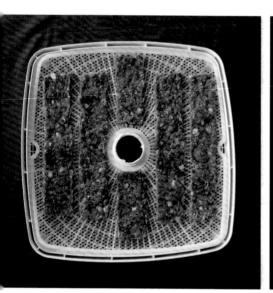

This is somewhat like pemmican because it's a meal in a stick. Either use half lean and half fat ground meat or about 85 percent lean. If there's a question, create the mixture and dry one or two pieces, taste-test, and make adjustments. Canned yams can be substituted for squash. It's important to drain the corn and squash of any extra liquid, otherwise the mixture becomes too thin.

FOR 2 pounds ground beef

2 teaspoons sea salt • ½ cup tamari • 3 tablespoons olive oil • 2 teaspoons ground sage • 1 teaspoon black pepper • ¾ cup cooked corn • ¾ cup cooked squash • ¾ cup canned pork and beans, lightly chopped

FOR 6 pounds ground beef

 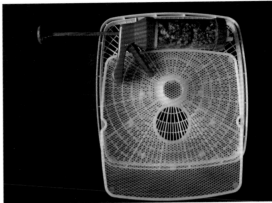

2 tablespoons sea salt • 1 cup tamari • ¼ cup olive oil • 3 tablespoons ground sage • 1 tablespoon black pepper, freshly ground • 2½ cups canned pork and beans, lightly chopped • 2¼ cups cooked corn • 2¼ cups cooked squash

Put meat and salt in a bowl and use a potato masher to force the salt into the meat. Lightly chop the beans so they're more easily extruded with a jerky gun. Combine all the other ingredients in a bowl and then wait a few minutes for the flavors to blend. Add to mixture. Put in a covered container or a self-sealing plastic bag. If marinating longer than 1 hour, place in the refrigerator. Because cold meat is harder to put through a jerky gun, let the mixture warm up for a few minutes before forming into strips and putting it in a drying environment.

BLACK BEAN SALSA JERKY

Try making this jerky with rehydrated dried mangoes, substitute coconut oil for olive oil, and add a dash of hot pepper.

1 pound ground beef

1 teaspoon onion salt • ½ cup black beans, lightly chopped • ¾ cup tomato-based salsa • 2 tablespoons Bragg Liquid Aminos • 1 tablespoon honey • 1 tablespoon olive oil • 1 tablespoon dried cilantro • 1 teaspoon cumin • ¼ teaspoon black pepper, freshly ground

Put meat, salt, and beans in a bowl and use a potato masher to force the salt into the meat. Combine all the other ingredients and then wait a few minutes for the flavors to blend. Add the salted ground meat and beans and thoroughly mix. Put in a covered container or a self-sealing plastic bag. If marinating longer than 1 hour, place in the refrigerator. Because cold meat is harder to put through a jerky gun, let the mixture warm up for a few minutes before forming into strips. If you use a jerky gun, the chunks may get stuck and you might need to use a knife or the flat side of a spoon to flatten out the strips. After putting in a drying environment, sprinkle with salt.

SPICY TOMATO SOY JERKY

Betsy Oman, a fellow drying enthusiast, has made lots of ground meat jerky and likes the way the tomato sauce absorbs fat.

1 pound ground meat

1 teaspoon salt • ⅓ cup tomato sauce • ¼ cup soy sauce • 2 tablespoons Worcestershire sauce • 1 tablespoon white wine vinegar • 1 tablespoon brown sugar • 1 teaspoon onion, finely chopped • 1 teaspoon garlic powder • 1 teaspoon black pepper, freshly ground • 1 teaspoon horseradish, grated fresh • ½ teaspoon Tabasco sauce • ¼ teaspoon liquid smoke

Put meat and salt in a bowl and use a potato masher to force the salt into the meat. Combine all the other ingredients in a bowl and then wait a few minutes for the flavors to blend. Add the salted ground meat and thoroughly mix. Put in a covered container or a self-sealing plastic bag. If marinating longer than 1 hour, place in the refrigerator. Because cold meat is harder to put through a jerky gun, let the mixture warm up for a few minutes before forming into strips and putting in a drying environment.

CHEESY JERKY

Most cheese would add too much oil to jerky, but with a dry cheese, like Parmesan, you get a lot of flavor. Charlie Trotter owned a famous restaurant in Chicago, and that's where we were first served dried blue cheese. For variety, add 2 teaspoons crushed dried tomato pieces and 1 teaspoon oregano or small pieces of dried papaya.

1 pound ground meat

1 teaspoon salt • 1 cup grated Parmesan cheese • 3 tablespoons soy sauce • 2 tablespoons dried blue cheese • 1 tablespoon olive oil • 1 teaspoon minced garlic • 1 teaspoon dried basil • ½ teaspoon black pepper, freshly ground • ¼ teaspoon liquid smoke

Put meat and salt in a bowl and use a potato masher to force the salt into the meat. Combine all the other ingredients in a bowl and then wait a few minutes for the flavors to blend. Add the salted ground meat and thoroughly mix. Put in a covered container or a self-sealing plastic bag. If marinating longer than 1 hour, place in the refrigerator. Because cold meat is harder to put through a jerky gun, let the mixture warm up for a few minutes before forming into strips and putting in a drying environment.

TIPSY JERKY

Triple sec gives this jerky a fruity flavor. Feel free to vary the alcohol to satisfy your taste buds.

1 pound ground meat

2 teaspoons celery salt • ½ cup dried mangoes, cut in small pieces • 1 tablespoon dried onions • ⅔ cup triple sec • 1 tablespoon lemon juice, fresh squeezed • 2 tablespoons honey • 1 tablespoon soy sauce • 1 tablespoon olive oil • ¼ teaspoon black pepper, freshly ground

Put meat and salt in a bowl and use a potato masher to force the salt into the meat. In a separate container, rehydrate mangoes and onions with the triple sec and lemon juice. Wait at least 30 minutes for the mangoes to rehydrate and then give a quick twirl in a blender to make smaller pieces. Meanwhile combine the honey, soy sauce, olive oil, and pepper in a bowl and then wait for the flavors to blend. Add the salted ground meat and rehydrated mangos and onions and thoroughly mix. Put in a covered container or a self-sealing plastic bag. If marinating longer than 1 hour, place in the refrigerator. Because cold meat is harder to put through a jerky gun, let the mixture warm up for a few minutes before forming into strips and putting in a drying environment.

TACO JERKY

Making taco jerky can be as simple as mixing meat with a commercial taco seasoning mix and ½ cup salsa. To make this recipe, you need to first dry the cheddar cheese on a leather tray. Be prepared to use paper towels to eliminate the excess oil. The jalapeño in this recipe was mild because I did not include the pith or seeds. Taste the marinade ingredients and, if it's not hot enough, add the seeds and pith.

1 pound ground meat

1 teaspoon sea salt • ⅓ cup Braggs Liquid Aminos • 3 tablespoons dried cheddar cheese • 1 tablespoon olive oil • 1 tablespoon dried tomato, broken into small pieces • 1 tablespoon jalapeño pepper, chopped fine • ½ teaspoon onion powder • ½ teaspoon cumin • ½ teaspoon chili powder • ¼ teaspoon dried chipotle pepper, Mexican if possible

Put meat and salt in a bowl and use a potato masher to force the salt into the meat. Combine all the other ingredients in a bowl and then wait a few minutes for the flavors to blend. Add the salted ground meat and thoroughly mix. Put in a covered container or a self-sealing plastic bag. If marinating longer than 1 hour, place in the refrigerator. Because cold meat is harder to put through a jerky gun, let the mixture warm up for a few minutes before forming into strips and putting in a drying environment.

MARY'S WHISKEY JERKY

When I handed a friend a strip of this jerky, she replied, "What could be better than booze and a hunk of meat?" Use any type of wild meat and vary the booze. Try rum, scotch whiskey, or brandy.

1 pound ground meat

1 teaspoon salt • 2 cups whiskey • 1 tablespoon soy sauce • 1 tablespoon brown sugar • 1 teaspoon oil • 1 teaspoon minced garlic, minced • ½ teaspoon black peppercorns, crushed • ¼ teaspoon liquid smoke

Put meat and salt in a bowl and use a potato masher to force the salt into the meat. Reduce whiskey to ½ cup in a pan with high sides to prevent the fumes from flaming. Note that if a flame appears, it will subside when the alcohol is gone. Add remaining ingredients to the whiskey with the exception of ground meat. Add the salted ground meat and thoroughly mix. Put in a covered container or a self-sealing plastic bag. If marinating longer than 1 hour, place in the refrigerator. Because cold meat is harder to put through a jerky gun, let the mixture warm up for a few minutes before forming into strips and putting in a drying environment.

BARBECUE JERKY

In the South, Coca-Cola is oftentimes added to a barbecue sauce. In the Rocky Mountains, Coors beer is a popular ingredient. Maple syrup is used in the upper Midwest. Hot peppers are included in the Southwest. To make a simple barbecue jerky, you can use a commercial sauce straight from the bottle and doctor it up with more chili and cayenne powder.

FOR 1 pound ground meat

1 teaspoon salt • 2 cups canned tomatoes • 1 tablespoon butter • ½ cup onion, chopped and cooked • 3 tablespoons brown sugar • 1 tablespoon cider vinegar • 2 teaspoons light molasses • 1 teaspoon smoked paprika • 1 teaspoon liquid smoke • 1 teaspoon onion powder • ½ teaspoon celery seed • ½ teaspoon cumin • ½ teaspoon dried mustard • ½ teaspoon black pepper, freshly ground

FOR 5 pounds ground meat

2 tablespoons salt • 8 cups canned tomatoes • 2 tablespoons butter • 2 cups onion, chopped and cooked • 1 cup brown sugar • ⅓ cup cider vinegar • 3 tablespoons light molasses • 2 tablespoons liquid smoke • 2 teaspoons onion powder • 2 teaspoons smoked paprika • 2 teaspoons celery seed • 1 teaspoon cumin • 1 teaspoon dry mustard • 1 teaspoon black pepper, freshly ground

Put meat into a bowl and use a potato masher to combine the salt. Put tomatoes in a pan and reduce to ½ cup. Sauté onions in butter until they turn light brown and add to the reduced tomatoes. Add other ingredients, except meat. Allow the ingredients at least 15 minutes for flavors to blend. Add ground meat. Marinate at least 1 hour. For longer marinating time, place in the refrigerator in a covered container or in an airtight plastic bag. Because cold meat is harder to put through a jerky gun, let the mixture warm up for a few minutes before forming into strips and putting in a drying environment.

RED WINE JERKY

For a little zip, add 1 tablespoon lemon juice and 1 teaspoon of freshly grated ginger.

1 pound ground meat

2 teaspoons salt • 1 cup red wine • ½ cup onion, chopped • 1 tablespoon olive oil • 2 teaspoons brown sugar • 1 tablespoon fresh basil, chopped • 1 teaspoon garlic, minced • ½ teaspoon black pepper, freshly ground • ½ teaspoon liquid smoke

Put meat into a bowl and use a potato masher to combine the salt. In a saucepan over medium-high heat, reduce wine to ½ cup. In a skillet, sauté onion in olive oil until lightly browned over medium-high heat. Add reduced wine and allow it to heat until it just begins to boil. Remove from heat. Add remaining ingredients except meat. Allow the ingredients at least 15 minutes for flavors to blend. Allow it to cool before pouring it into blender. Blend and add to meat. Marinate at least 1 hour. For longer marinating time, place in the refrigerator in a covered container or in an airtight plastic bag. Remove from marinade container. Because cold meat is harder to put through a jerky gun, let the mixture warm up for a few minutes before forming into strips and putting in a drying environment.

RHUBARB JERKY

My town of Lanesboro, Minnesota, is the Rhubarb Capitol of Minnesota. Our motto is Live Local—Live Well. Every year on the first Saturday of June, our little town of 750 swells to several thousand people who come to experience rhubarb. Even Garrison Keillor was drawn to this event and broadcast an episode of *Prairie Home Companion* during the festival. The big event is the taste-testing contest, and in 2016 the Rhubarb Jerky took first place.

Feel free to substitute raisins for Craisins, but they must be ground small enough to fit through the nozzle of a jerky gun.

3 pounds ground meat

3 pounds rhubarb, to make 6 cups rhubarb purée • 3 teaspoons salt • ¼ cup dried onions, minced • 2 tablespoons lemon juice, freshly squeezed • 3 teaspoons ground allspice • 1 cup Craisins, finely chopped • ½ cup honey
• 1 teaspoon black pepper

To prepare the rhubarb, cut into ½-inch pieces, wash, put in a pot, and pour enough boiling water to cover, then cover with a lid. Let it sit until the color changes and the rhubarb is soft to the touch. This blanching does

two things: it removes some of the acid so it will require less sweetener and it will be easier to purée. Drain rhubarb and purée in a blender. Spread 4 cups on a lightly oiled leather sheet and dry until it can be crumbled or ground into flakes—this may take several hours.

Put meat and salt in a bowl and use a potato masher to force the salt into the meat. Combine onions with 2 cups of rhubarb purée, rehydrate 10 minutes, and then add the remaining ingredients. When the rhubarb sauce is dry, either crush by hand or give it a twirl in a blender. Thoroughly mix the flavored meat with the dried rhubarb. Put in a covered container or a self-sealing plastic bag. If marinating longer than 1 hour, place in the refrigerator. Because cold meat is harder to put through a jerky gun, let the mixture warm up for a few minutes before forming into strips and putting in a drying environment.

HERB JERKY

Although this marinade contains mainly dried herbs, feel free to substitute finely chopped fresh herbs. To add more flavor, add ½ teaspoon crushed red peppers and ½ teaspoon Tabasco sauce.

1 pound ground meat

1 teaspoon salt • ⅓ cup white wine • 1 tablespoon olive oil • 1 tablespoon lemon juice • 1 tablespoon Worcestershire sauce • 1 tablespoon honey • 1 tablespoon onion, grated • 1 teaspoon dried basil • 1 teaspoon dried oregano • 1 teaspoon garlic, minced • 1 teaspoon black pepper, freshly ground • ½ teaspoon dried rosemary, crushed

Put meat into a bowl and use a potato masher to combine the salt. Mix all ingredients together with the exception of salted ground meat. Allow the ingredients at least 15 minutes for flavors to blend. Add ground meat. Marinate at least 1 hour. For longer marinating time, place in the refrigerator in a covered container or in an airtight plastic bag. Because cold meat is harder to put through a jerky gun, let the mixture warm up for a few minutes before forming into strips and putting in a drying environment.

ONION JERKY

This jerky feels like strip jerky because onions add a lot of texture. In fact, taste-testers could not tell this was made with ground meat. If you don't want to chop onions, buy a 2-ounce package of dried onion soup mix and add 1 teaspoon water and 2 tablespoons teriyaki sauce.

1 pound ground meat

1 teaspoon salt • 2 cups onion, finely chopped • ¼ cup butter • 2 tablespoons brown sugar • 3 tablespoons tamari • 1 tablespoon Worcestershire sauce • 1 tablespoon garlic, roasted and mashed • ¼ cup raw onion, grated • ½ teaspoon onion powder • ¼ teaspoon black pepper, freshly ground

Put meat into a bowl and use a potato masher to combine the salt. Place onions in a sauté pan over high heat and add butter. Sauté and then add brown sugar to caramelize. Stir to avoid burning and sauté until onions turn a rich caramel color. Remove from heat. Purée and add the other ingredients, except meat. Allow the ingredients at least 15 minutes for flavors to blend. Add ground meat. Marinate at least 1 hour. For longer marinating time, place in the refrigerator in a covered container or in an airtight plastic bag. Because cold meat is harder to put through a jerky gun, let the mixture warm up for a few minutes before forming into strips and putting in a drying environment.

HOT JERKY

For those who want their lips to sweat, substitute a habanero for the jalapeño. This jerky can be made super hot by adding 1 teaspoon of sriracha.

1 pound ground meat

1 teaspoon sea salt • ⅓ cup teriyaki sauce • 2 tablespoons jalapeño peppers, seeded and finely chopped • 1 tablespoon olive oil • 1 tablespoon garlic, minced • 1 tablespoon horseradish, freshly ground • 2 teaspoons white sugar • 2 teaspoons black pepper, freshly ground • ½ teaspoon paprika • ½ teaspoon chili powder • ¼ teaspoon Tabasco sauce

Put meat and salt in a bowl and use a potato masher to force the salt into the meat. Combine all the other ingredients in a bowl and then wait a few minutes for the flavors to blend. Add the salted ground meat and thoroughly mix. Put in a covered container or a self-sealing plastic bag. If marinating longer than 1 hour, place in the refrigerator. Because cold meat is harder to put through a jerky gun, let the mixture warm up for a few minutes before forming into strips and putting in a drying environment.

SAGE JERKY

Buffalo is low in fat, calories, and cholesterol and high in protein, iron, and thiamine. This "Wisdom Jerky" is intended to honor the spiritual nature of the buffalo and sage.

1 pound ground buffalo

1 teaspoon Himalayan pink salt • 2 tablespoons maple syrup • 1 tablespoon apple cider vinegar • 1 tablespoon soy sauce • 1 tablespoon olive oil • 2 teaspoons ground sage • 1 teaspoon lemon juice, freshly squeezed • ¼ teaspoon ground cardamom

Put meat and salt in a bowl and use a potato masher to force the salt into the meat. Combine all the other ingredients in a bowl and then wait a few minutes for the flavors to blend. Add the salted ground meat and thoroughly mix. Put in a covered container or a self-sealing plastic bag. If marinating longer than 1 hour, place in the refrigerator. Because cold meat is harder to put through a jerky gun, let the mixture warm up for a few minutes before forming into strips and putting in a drying environment. Sprinkle a little salt or fresh ground pepper over the strips.

GOAT JERKY

Although goat is not as commonly eaten in the United States, around the world it is one of the most used protein sources. Taste-testers especially liked the caraway flavor and the dried sauerkraut was surprising. If you choose to add fresh sauerkraut, use 1 cup.

1 pound ground goat

1 teaspoon Himalayan pink salt • 1½ tablespoons coconut oil • ½ cup brown sugar • ½ cup dried sauerkraut • 1 teaspoon black peppercorns, coarsely ground • 1 teaspoon caraway seeds, crushed

Put goat and salt in a bowl and use a potato masher to combine the salt. Add coconut oil, brown sugar, sauerkraut, peppercorns, and caraway seeds and mash until well blended. Marinate at least 1 hour. For longer marinating time, place in the refrigerator in a covered container or in an airtight plastic bag. Because cold meat is harder to put through a jerky gun, let the mixture warm up for a few minutes before forming into strips and putting in a drying environment.

LAMB JERKY

At a family gathering, I had the chance to talk with a relative who was originally from Tunisia. She shared her 1,400-year-old jerky recipe. She said lamb was always ground twice to make sure there were no lumps. Her family added garlic, cracked pepper, and mint and used their hands to mix the meat. She said a royal treat was to add pine nuts to the mixture.

1 pound ground lamb

1 teaspoon salt • ½ cup onion, finely chopped • ⅓ cup orange juice • 2 tablespoons honey • 2 tablespoons olive oil • 1 tablespoon fresh mint, finely chopped • 1 teaspoon cinnamon • ½ teaspoon black pepper, freshly ground • ¼ teaspoon cayenne pepper • ¼ teaspoon nutmeg

Put lamb and salt in a bowl and use a potato masher to combine the salt. Sauté onion, orange juice, and honey over high heat. Cook until brown. Remove from heat. Add all ingredients except lamb. Cool. Allow the ingredients at least 15 minutes for flavors to blend. Add ground lamb. Marinate at least 1 hour. For longer marinating time, place in the refrigerator in a covered container or in an airtight plastic bag. Because cold meat is harder to put through a jerky gun, let the mixture warm up for a few minutes before forming into strips and putting in a drying environment.

CURRIED TURKEY JERKY

People like to say "Turkey Jerky," and then laugh and smack their lips. This jerky tends to crumble instead of sticking together, but has a truly wonderful taste. We like to crush it and add to our salads.

1 pound ground turkey

1 teaspoon salt • ½ cup crushed pineapple • 2 tablespoons coconut oil • 1 tablespoon honey • 1 teaspoon ginger, freshly ground • 1 teaspoon curry powder • ½ teaspoon lemon peel, fresh grated • ¼ teaspoon black pepper, freshly ground

Put turkey into a bowl and use a potato masher to combine the salt. Mix all ingredients together with the exception of salted ground meat. Allow the ingredients at least 15 minutes for flavors to blend. Add ground meat. Marinate at least 1 hour. For longer marinating time, place in the refrigerator in a covered container or in an airtight plastic bag. Because cold meat is harder to put through a jerky gun, let the mixture warm up for a few minutes before forming into strips and putting in a drying environment.

A SILVER LINING

Mike Schafer owns Schafer Fisheries in Fulton, Illinois, just across the Mississippi River from Clinton, Iowa, at US Lock and Dam #13. His family-owned-and-operated business began in 1976.

In 1993, Mike was looking for new ways to expand his business. At this time, Asian carp were infiltrating the Mississippi River. In April 1997, *Big River* magazine wrote an article called "Camp Kielbasa" that talked about how Mike was starting to create a silver carp jerky recipe. "That article gave me incentive to go forward," he said. "It took years for me to develop a jerky I liked and it soon became our main product."

Mike has been a pioneer in the Asian carp industry and has helped turn the carp invasion into a valuable protein source. "With a worldwide need for protein, this fish could feed a lot of people," he said.

Silver carp are known to leap from the water and jump right into boats. They also compete with the native fish and disrupt the ecosystem. "By removing this fish, it can help control and replenish native fish stocks," Mike said proudly. "They are as fast as sharks, have the highest quality collagen in the skins, the flesh is white. They are vegetarians and not bottom feeders, like other carp. Plus there's no shortage of these fish. It takes regular carp about 10 years to reach 25 pounds, but the Asian carp can get that big in four years."

Mike's 30,000-foot plant processes 30 million pounds of fish per year. Schafer Fisheries uses all parts of the fish and sells it as organic fertilizer. To make jerky, he first presses carp fillets through heavy-duty screens to remove the needle-thin bones. "But because this fish has little fat, it needs a binder to form it into a jerky." Then he warned, "Be careful about adding too much extra liquid." To finish his jerky, he puts it in a smoker. "I don't use hickory because it makes jerky dark. Depending on the humidity, sometimes it can take two days to finish."

MIKE'S CARPE DIEM JERKY

Wild caught, flying Asian carp easily takes on other flavors," Mike said. If you want to minimize the fishy taste, increase the adobo to 2 teaspoons. Feel free to substitute minced carp for any recipe that calls for turkey or any other ground meat. Adding cheese helped this jerky stick together and yet stay flexible.

1 pound Asian carp, minced

2 teaspoons sea salt • ⅔ cup instant mashed potatoes • ¾ cup sharp cheddar cheese, shredded • 1 tablespoon lime juice, freshly squeezed • 2 teaspoons honey • 1 heaping teaspoon lime zest • 1 teaspoon adobo spice • 1 teaspoon cumin • ½ teaspoon black pepper, freshly ground • ½ teaspoon garlic powder

Put minced carp into a colander and let drain for 30 minutes. Then put in a bowl, add salt, and force it into the fish with a potato masher. Put it back in the colander and drain another 30 minutes. Combine the rest of the ingredients and add to the fish. Stir. Marinate at least 1 hour. For longer marinating time, place in the refrigerator in a covered container or in an airtight plastic bag. Because cold material is harder to put through a jerky gun, let the mixture warm up for a few minutes before forming into strips and putting in a drying environment.

CRAPPIE JERKY

This is a marvelous combination of both fish and tartar sauce. Feel free to use any other mild fish fillets. To mince, chop the semi-thawed fillets into big chunks and give a twirl in a food processor.

1 pound crappie fillets, minced

1 teaspoon sea salt • 3 tablespoons butter • 1½ cups zucchini, peeled, cut ¼-inch pieces • 2 tablespoons dill pickles, minced • 2 tablespoons sweet pickles, minced • 1 tablespoon lemon juice • 1 tablespoon brown sugar • 1 teaspoon onion powder • 1 teaspoon white vinegar • 2 teaspoons heavy cream • ½ teaspoon ground mustard • ¼ teaspoon freshly ground black pepper • ¼ teaspoon garlic powder • ½ cup panko bread crumbs • 1 teaspoon cornmeal

Mix minced crappie with salt in a bowl and set aside. In a large skillet, melt 2 tablespoons butter over medium heat and add peeled zucchini and sauté until soft but not brown. Cool and purée the zucchini. Combine zucchini, pickles, and fish. Stir then add all the remaining ingredients with the exception of bread crumbs and cornmeal.

Over medium-high heat, melt the remaining tablespoon of butter in a skillet. Add bread crumbs and cornmeal and toast until golden. Remove from heat and cool for a couple minutes before adding to the fish mixture. Marinate at least 1 hour. For longer marinating time, place in the refrigerator in a covered container or in an airtight plastic bag. Because cold material is harder to put through a jerky gun, let the mixture warm up for a few minutes before forming into strips and putting in a drying environment.

VEGETARIAN JERKY

If you or your friends like the idea of jerky but have decided not to eat meat, here's a great recipe to try. Most commercial vegetarian jerkies use various forms of a vegetable protein (TVP) made from defatted, cooked soy flour. It's available in flakes, chunks, and moist options.

I used a moist soy protein that contained no fat or cholesterol, was low in sodium, and high in protein, fiber, and iron. It contained purified water, soy protein, dehydrated onion, dehydrated red bell pepper, carrageenan, modified vegetable gum, and caramel coloring (from corn syrup). Its texture was similar to raw hamburger.

To use soy protein, you need a thickening or mucilaginous agent to hold it together during the drying process to get a jerk-like texture. Cooked oatmeal, mashed potatoes, and applesauce serve as bonding agents. Packaged instant oatmeal is the quickest and easiest. Add ¼ cup water to a 1½-ounce instant oatmeal package, stir until it thickens, and then mix it with the other ingredients. My breakthrough came with caramelizing onions, and the result was a jerky with a strip-like texture.

You can use all of the marinades in both the strip and ground meat sections to make it flavorful. The longer flavors are allowed to blend, the better the flavor.

When making vegetarian jerky, the drying temperature is not as important as when making other jerkies. Note that vegetarian jerky dries crisp like a cracker. If it becomes too crisp, you can soak it again in a light marinade for a few minutes and dry again. Then you can put it in a smoky environment for 1 hour to add more flavor.

Vegetarian jerky can be made with tofu. Cut tofu into 1-inch by 2-inch slabs about ¼ inch thick. Soak overnight in your choice of a marinade. Dried tofu jerky is a bit rubbery, but a worthwhile protein source on a backpacking trip.

TASTES-LIKE-MEAT JERKY

My goal in making a vegetable jerky was to come up with one that people thought was meat. All my testers said they couldn't tell that it wasn't meat. Success!

1 pound soy protein

½ cup raw onion, finely grated • 2 tablespoons brown sugar • ½ tablespoon garlic, minced • 1 tablespoon soy sauce • 1 teaspoon black pepper, freshly ground • 1 teaspoon salt • 1 tablespoon hot pepper • 1 tablespoon olive oil • 1 tablespoon rum • ½ teaspoon liquid smoke • 1 tablespoon raw green bell pepper, grated • 1 package (1½ ounces) instant oatmeal • ¼ cup water

Caramelize onions in brown sugar. When browned, add garlic and remove from heat. Add next eight ingredients. Stir and allow flavors to blend at least 15 minutes. Mix oatmeal and water and add to soy protein. Mix flavorings and soy protein together. Marinate at least 1 hour. Remove from marinating container, form into shapes, and place in a drying environment.

CHAPTER 7
Using Jerky

Cooking and baking with jerky is simple. It can add extremely flavorful and sometimes seemingly outrageous ingredients to a swath of various recipes. Jerky is a potent ingredient because the marinating process imparts a lot of flavor to the meat.

Sometimes people seem surprised when I suggest adding a handful of jerky to a soup or stew. How about using jerky instead of commercial bacon bits? Add pizzazz to pizza, spaghetti sauce, or a casserole, or toss jerky into a soup, hash, rice, or omelet.

In addition, jerky is right up there when it comes to fat-free and healthy since only lean meats are used. When you choose wild or grass-fed animals, you can create chemical- and hormone-free jerkies.

When a recipe's instructions call for rehydrating (soaking) jerky, I generally use about ½ cup liquid per 1 cup jerky. Wine, vegetable juices, and fruit juices, even liquors are great rehydration liquids. Depending on the size of pieces, the amount of time it takes jerky to rehydrate can vary from a few minutes to an hour. Small pieces and warm rehydration liquids will shorten the rehydration time. When adding jerky to dishes that have adequate liquid, there's no need to rehydrate, but do allow a little time for the jerky to swell up.

Any of the recipes in this chapter can be used with ground or strip jerky. A slow cooker is a great appliance for rehydrating jerky recipes. Oftentimes, the jerkies I use in recipes are the result of a too tough or too dry batch—in other words, they're from a somewhat failed attempt.

Ground meat jerky can easily be broken apart with your fingers or cut with a sharp knife, kitchen shears, an electric slicer, or can be placed in a blender to make a powder. It's best to cut jerky into small pieces before putting in a blender, and you should only grind a small amount at a time. Jerky can be ground coarse or fine. A 1-inch-wide strip that's about 5 inches long becomes about 1 tablespoon of jerky powder.

Historically, the Celts of Armorica and the nomads of Asia Minor mixed small pieces of jerky with hot water and drank it much like we do coffee. In 1680, a guy by the name of Martin made a drink from powdered jerky and water and it became known as Martin's Broth. More recently, American cowboys were known to put a hunk of the old-time jerky under their saddles and ride until it got soft enough to chew.

PEMMICAN

TRADITIONAL PEMMICAN

Traditional pemmican is a high-protein, calorie-rich, concentrated, portable snack food. It not only nourished Native Americans, but it also served as a staple for pioneers as they ventured westward.

Wasna is the Sioux word for pemmican. It's a combination of powdered or finely chopped dried meats, dried berries, and animal fat mixed into a thick paste and then stuffed into airtight animal skins. It has been made from a variety of wild game, including buffalo, venison, beef, moose, beaver, antelope, elk, rabbit, and fish, and has contained a variety of wild fruits, such as strawberries, blueberries, huckleberries, raspberries, chokecherries, buffalo berries, and wild plums. Along with a handful of dried rose hips (vitamin C), pemmican is an almost complete life-sustaining portable food. In other words, pemmican is a kind of portable mincemeat.

In the late 1700s, Pembina, North Dakota, was the Native American commercial center for pemmican. In the early1800s, when trade reached its peak, various fillers such as oatmeal and potato flour were added as well as various dried vegetables.

Dakota Pemmican Mallet

You can use a mortar and pestle to grind jerky into a powder. A special one-faced hammer called a pemmican mallet was a useful tool for Native Americans.

The very first pemmican recipe I found began with, "Cut up one elk." After cracked bones were boiled in water, the rich, sweet, salty butter-like fat was skimmed off and used to make pemmican. Alternatively, animal fat was cut into small (1-inch) chunks, heated in a pan over a slow fire, but never allowed to boil. Warmed fat was easier to combine with the other ingredients. Pemmican was left to cool and thicken into a paste before being stuffed into animal intestine casings that had been soaked in salted water at least 1 hour prior to stuffing. The ends were then tied off.

SIMPLE PEMMICAN

"I like eating jerky and apple leather together," Glenda Ohs chuckled. "So one day I scratched my head and thought, why not put them together?"

While jerky is still a little tacky, spoon a thin layer of applesauce on top and dry until it is no longer sticky, then turn the jerky over and coat the other side and then continue with the drying process.

MODERN PEMMICAN

Pemmican can be made with either strip or ground meat jerky. Grind a few small pieces of jerky at one time in the blender. The smaller the pieces, the easier it will be to chew. I use peanut butter instead of fat, and oatmeal acts as a binder. Depending on the desired product, you can either cook or not cook the oatmeal—uncooked, it becomes more like a meat granola bar. For variety, add chopped nuts or dried apples, pineapple, peaches, prunes, or raisins. Makes 12 (1-inch by 4-inch) strips.

1 cup jerky, coarsely ground

¼ cup butter • 2 tablespoons honey • 1 cup creamy peanut butter • ¾ cup oatmeal • ⅓ cup dried blueberries • ⅓ cup dried apricots, chopped small • ⅓ cup dried cherries, chopped small • ⅓ cup dried cranberries • ¼ teaspoon black pepper, freshly ground

Melt butter in a fry pan and add jerky. Stir for 1 minute and then add honey, peanut butter, and oatmeal. Let rest for a few minutes and then add the remaining ingredients. Lightly oil a 12-by-12-inch baking pan. Pour the mixture in and press down to flatten, and then cut into cubes or strips. Or spread the mixture onto a sheet of plastic wrap and firmly pull it around to compress the pemmican into a log shape. Or make into balls and roll in coconut.

JERKY PARFLECHES

A *parfleche* is a Native American rawhide bag, like a purse, suitcase, or enve-lope that was used for holding personal belongings and dried food. This recipe was inspired by the menu offering Savory Purse of American Bison and Wisconsin Wild Plum at the restaurant L'Etoile in Madison, Wisconsin. Makes 8 entrée-size pouches or 24 individual appetizers.

1 cup jerky, coarsely chopped

1 cup orange juice concentrate • ½ cup dried cranberries • ½ cup dried blueberries • ½ cup dried cherries, cut small • ½ cup dried apricots, cut small • 1 tablespoons red wine vinegar • 1 tablespoon rice vinegar • 1 teaspoon lemon juice • 1 teaspoon fresh thyme, finely chopped • 1 teaspoon fresh rosemary, finely chopped • 1 tablespoon olive oil • 30 (12- by-17-inch) phyllo sheets • 1 cup butter, melted • ½ cup bread crumbs • 2 cups wild plum sauce

Rehydrate the jerky in orange juice for at least 15 minutes. Combine the rest of the ingredients in the listing down to the olive oil. Set aside and allow at least 1 hour for the flavors to blend. In a saucepan, heat olive oil and add the rehydrated jerky and then add the combined ingredients. Simmer slowly, stirring often.

Place the phyllo sheets on a clean, dry work surface. Depending on the intended servings, you can determine what shape to cut the sheets so they become pocket-like shapes.

Lightly oil a cookie sheet. With each layer, brush a light coat of butter, starting at edges and then painting the center. Sprinkle a pinch of bread crumbs over the sheet to help keep the phyllo light and flaky. Build at least five layers in this manner. Then place at least 1 rounded tablespoon of the jerky mixture in the center of each square. Brush butter on the phyllo so that when you pinch the corners together, they stick to form a "purse." Use melted butter to bind the edges together and brush the top of each parfleche with a little butter before putting it in the oven. Bake 15 to 20 minutes at 400 degrees until the tops are golden. If desired, cook sliced plums over medium heat until a sauce forms. Simmer the plum sauce and then drizzle over each individual parfleche.

Everyday Cooking with Jerky

JERKY BOUILLON

The Oberto Jerky company packages "jerky dust" and suggests adding it to salads, soups, and sauces. You can, of course, use your own ground jerky. Makes 1 cup.

⅓ cup powdered jerky • 1 cup hot water

Mix jerky and water together and allow at least 15 minutes to rehydrate. Uncooked, rehydrated jerky should be refrigerated if not used within 1 hour.

DEER SOUP

Cooking with jerky is not new. The Native American community has long known the value of adding it to a kettle of dried corn, squash, and beans. This original recipe was called Na'le Shik'usna: dap K'yabiomowe Woley-anne. Serves 6 to 8.

2 cups venison jerky, cut into bite-sized pieces • 8 cups water • 2 tablespoons oil • 4 cups potatoes, peeled and cubed

Put venison in a pan with water and add oil. Cook until almost tender and add potatoes. Feel free add any dried foods, like turnips or squash (pictured above), and flavor with pepper, garlic, onion, or coriander.

JERKY DIP

Any jerky, including fish, can be used in this recipe. Serve with crackers, potato chips, raw vegetables, dried tomato chips, or put on top of a baked potato. For variety, add 1 tablespoon roasted garlic and 1 teaspoon dried tomato powder.

½ cup jerky, cut in ¼-inch pieces

2 tablespoons water • 1 tablespoon butter • ½ cup pecans, chopped • 1 teaspoon onion powder • ½ cup green olives, chopped • 1 (8-ounce) package cream cheese, softened • ½ cup sour cream • 1 teaspoon lemon juice • 1 teaspoon red pepper, finely chopped

In a bowl, combine jerky and water and let sit at least 15 minutes. Melt butter, add rehydrated jerky, and simmer over low heat. When the liquid evaporates, add pecans and onion power and simmer a few minutes. Add cream cheese, sour cream, and lemon juice. Mix thoroughly. Put in a bowl lined with plastic wrap and refrigerate at least 1 hour to give the flavors a chance to blend. Top with red pepper and serve with crackers.

JERKY PUFFS

Ground meat jerky works best, although any type of jerky can be used to make this party appetizer. Makes 24.

¼ cup ground jerky, broken into small pieces

¼ cup water • 1 tablespoon butter • 2 egg whites • ½ cup cheddar cheese, shredded • ¼ cup mayonnaise • ⅛ teaspoon black pepper, freshly ground • 24 crackers • paprika to sprinkle

Put jerky and water in a bowl and allow it to rehydrate at least 15 minutes. Then put it in a saucepan with butter and cook off any extra liquid. Let cool. Whip egg whites until stiff. Mix together jerky, cheese, mayonnaise, and pepper. Gently fold in the stiff egg whites. Place crackers on a cookie sheet and spoon a teaspoon of jerky mixture on each cracker. Place under the broiler for 2 minutes or until the tops turn golden brown. Serve hot.

JERKY SALAD

I like Curried Turkey Jerky (page 122) in this salad. We break it up into small pieces; it's something like adding flavorful bacon bits. Serves 2 to 4.

Dressing

1 cup olive oil • ⅔ cup rice vinegar • ⅓ cup white sugar • 3 tablespoons apple cider vinegar • 2 tablespoons Worcestershire sauce • 1 teaspoon salt • 1 teaspoon dry mustard

Salad

6 ounces mixed greens • 4 ounces blue cheese • 1 pear, cut in cubes • 1 avocado, cut in cubes • 4 green onions, sliced thin • 2 tablespoons almonds, sliced • ½ cup jerky, broken into small pieces

Blend the dressing. Mix together the salad and stir in jerky.

NILE'S JERKY OMELET

My brother-in-law, Nile Deden, is known for making great breakfasts, so when I shared a package of my Barbecue Jerky (page 64), he started cracking eggs. Serves 1.

2 tablespoons jerky pieces

1 tablespoon dried tomato pieces • 2 tablespoons water • 2 tablespoons onion, chopped • 2 teaspoons butter • 2 eggs • 1 tablespoon Parmesan cheese

Combine jerky, tomatoes, and water and let sit 30 minutes. Sauté onion in butter and add rehydrated jerky and tomatoes and cook over low heat until all liquid evaporates. Whip eggs and either make scrambled eggs or spoon the jerky mixture and make an omelet. Top with cheese.

MACHACHA NORTENA

Art Oberto believed that jerky was great to use in cooking. He shared his Spanish scrambled egg and shredded dried meat breakfast. Serves 6.

½ cup jerky, shredded

½ medium onion, finely chopped • 1 tablespoon oil • 3 chili peppers, finely chopped • 12 eggs, beaten • 6 flour tortillas

Lightly fry the onion in hot oil and add peppers. Add the jerky, stir, and add eggs. Stir constantly. When the eggs are cooked, remove from heat, and fill the tortillas.

JERKY HASH

This has been a family favorite and it will work with just about any type of jerky. Serves 4.

1 cup jerky, cut in small pieces

2 tablespoons dried onions • 1½ cups water • 4 cups half-cooked potatoes, cubed • ¼ cup celery, finely chopped • ¼ cup red pepper, finely chopped • 2 tablespoons green onions, chopped • 1 tablespoon rice vinegar • 1 teaspoon garlic, minced • 1 teaspoon fresh thyme, diced • ½ cup grated cheese • salt and pepper to taste

Rehydrate jerky and onions in water for 1 hour. Over medium heat, cook down the liquid to half and then add potatoes. Reduce heat and cook until potatoes soften. Add celery, pepper, green onions, vinegar, garlic, and thyme. Stir and top with cheese and salt and pepper.

HEARTY CHOWDER

While my friend Sue Schreur and I were traveling together in the South-west, we made this recipe and served it at a gathering with our Navajo friends. Everyone loved it. We used Sweet Jerky (page 53), but the Three Sisters (page 104) is another good choice. Serve with a loaf of Jerky Bread (page 153) and you've got it all. Serves 6.

1 cup jerky, cut in small pieces

2 cups water • 3 tablespoons butter • 1 cup onion, chopped • 1 tablespoon garlic, minced • 1 teaspoon ground cumin • 1 (15-ounce) can black beans, drained • 1 (15-ounce) can creamed corn • 2 cups frozen corn • 1 (4-ounce) can fire-roasted green chile • 2 tablespoons salsa verde • 1 cup cream • 1 cup milk • 2 cups Monterey Jack cheese, grated • ¼ teaspoon black pepper, freshly ground • garnish with cilantro, sliced fresh tomato, and avocado

Rehydrate jerky in water for at least 15 minutes. Put butter in a soup pot, melt, and add onions and garlic. Sauté and then add rehydrated jerky and cumin. Stir. Add beans, corns, chile, and salsa. Let simmer. Fifteen minutes before serving, add cream, milk, cheese, and pepper. Serve with cilantro, tomatoes, and avocadoes.

JERKED GOULASH

Although this recipe is especially good with beef, it also works well with poultry. This makes is a great backpacking meal. On the trail, once you reach your destination, add water, heat, and serve. Serves 2 to 4.

4 cups canned whole tomatoes • ½ cup jerky, cut in small pieces • 2 tablespoons olive oil • 1 cup onion, diced • 1 teaspoon garlic, minced • 1 teaspoon dried basil • 1 teaspoon dried oregano • 1 cup macaroni • salt and pepper to taste

Put tomatoes in a soup pot and squeeze with your hands. Add dried meat, stir, and rehydrate at least 30 minutes. Place oil, onions, garlic, basil, and oregano in a frying pan on high heat and stir until thoroughly cooked. Reduce heat to medium low and cook 5 to 10 minutes, longer if you need to cook off some of the liquid. Remove from heat and add to tomatoes. Cook pasta in a separate pan and then drain. Mix ingredients together.

CREAMED JERKY

Growing up in the 1950s, creamed chipped beef was a regular meal my mom served on toast. Just about any type of jerky can be shaved thin and substituted for store-bought chipped beef. Serve over toast, or muffins, cooked potatoes, rice, or pasta. Consider adding rehydrated dried mushrooms or green peas. Serves 2.

1 cup jerky

½ cup dry sherry • ½ cup onion, minced • 2 tablespoons butter • 1 tablespoon red pepper, minced • 1 heaping tablespoon flour • ¾ cup milk • ¾ cup cream • 2 teaspoons capers • 1 teaspoon dried parsley • 4 slices buttered toast

Rehydrate jerky in sherry and let sit 15 minutes. Put onions and butter in a saucepan and sauté until the onions are golden. Add pepper and rehydrated jerky. Stir. Sprinkle flour on top and stir constantly. Add milk and cream. Simmer until the sauce thickens. Remove from heat and add capers and parsley. Serve over toast.

JERKY QUICHE

I liked the idea of a mashed potatoes shell, and this is a good way to use leftovers. Serves 4.

¾ cup jerky, cut in small pieces

1½ cups half-and-half • ¾ cup dried kale • 1½ cups instant mashed potatoes, rehydrated • ⅓ cup butter • 1 cup mushrooms, diced • 1 tablespoon butter • 3 eggs, whipped • 1 cup cheddar cheese, shredded • ¼ teaspoon black pepper

Rehydrate jerky and kale in 1 cup of half-and-half for 15 minutes. Spoon the mashed potatoes into a 9-inch pie plate and line the bottom and sides. Bake at 325 degrees for 20 minutes or until it turns golden. Melt butter and sauté mushrooms. When cooked, add the jerky and kale mixture together. Simmer over low heat until liquid is absorbed. Remove from heat. In a bowl, whisk eggs and then add the remaining ½ cup half-and-half and half the cheese. Pour into potato-lined pie pan. Bake 30 to 40 minutes at 375 degrees. After removing from the oven, sprinkle the remaining cheese on top.

JERKY SLAW

My friend Jan Smart has made this colorful and yet simple recipe for her family for years, and she loved the Barbecue Jerky (page 64) addition. Serves 4.

½ cup of jerky, shaved thin

3 tablespoons olive oil • 2 tablespoons balsamic vinegar • 1 tablespoon lemon juice, freshly squeezed • ¼ teaspoon lemon zest • 1 tablespoon honey • 1 teaspoon sea salt • ¼ teaspoon pepper, freshly ground • 2 cups broccoli stems, sliced thin • ½ cup multicolored carrots, shaved thin • ¼ cup onion, chopped • ¼ cup red cabbage, sliced thin • 1 tablespoon red pepper, sliced thin

Put jerky in a bowl. Combine the oil, vinegar, lemon juice and zest, honey, salt and pepper, stir, and let rehydrate for at least 15 minutes. Combine the rest of the vegetables in a bowl and add the rehydrated jerky. Stir. Let flavors blend for at least 30 minutes.

SCALLOPED POTATOES AND JERKY

This is the kind of dish my family considers a comfort meal. Serves 4.

1 cup jerky, broken into small pieces

1½ cup water • 1 cup onion, chopped • 1 tablespoon olive oil • 1 cup mushrooms, chopped • 1 tablespoon butter • 1 heaping tablespoon flour • 1 cup cream • ¼ teaspoon celery seed • ¼ teaspoon black pepper, freshly ground • 6 medium-sized potatoes, peeled and sliced • 1 cup shredded cheese

Place jerky and ½ cup water together, stir, and let rehydrate at least 30 minutes. Sauté onions in olive oil. Then sauté mushrooms in butter. Combine onions and mushrooms. Whisk 1 cup water with flour and add to onions and mushrooms. Stir and then add cream, celery seed, and pepper. Spray a 1-quart casserole dish and begin layering the potatoes, then sauce, then cheese, until all the ingredients are added. Bake at 375 degrees for 1 hour.

PASTA CON CARNE SECA

Originally this simple, yet elegant main course was a recipe that Peter Beck shared with us. Over the years, it has had many incarnations and has been served at lots of special occasions. Serves 2.

1 cup jerky, coarsely ground

½ cup red wine • 2 cups mushrooms, sliced • 4 tablespoons butter • ¼ cup water • 1 cup cream • 2 cups cooked pasta • ½ teaspoon basil • ½ cup peas • ½ cup onion, chopped • 1 cup tomatoes, cubed • ½ cup Parmesan cheese, shredded • ½ teaspoon black pepper, coarsely ground

Put jerky into a bowl, add wine, and stir. Let sit at least 1 hour. Sauté mushrooms in half the butter. Place the rest of the butter into a frying pan and add the rehydrated jerky and brown. Add water and cream and stir. Remove from heat. Sauté mushrooms, reduce the heat, and add the meat mixture. Add pasta to jerky mixture. Add basil, peas, onions, and tomatoes and then top with Parmesan cheese and black pepper.

WINDY CHILI

This started out as spaghetti sauce, but the day was windy and cold and it turned into a "spaghetti, no, chili for a windy day" memory. Spicy Tomato Soy (page 107) is a good jerky to use in this chili. Serves 12.

1½ cups jerky, shredded

1 cup onion, chopped • 1 tablespoon oil • 1 teaspoon dried oregano • 1 teaspoon dried basil • 1 tablespoon garlic, minced • 1 cup celery, chopped • 1 cup green pepper, chopped • 4 cups V8 juice • 1½ teaspoons chili powder • 2 cups black beans • 2 cups chickpeas (garbanzo beans) • 2 cups kidney beans • 3 cups canned tomatoes • ¼ teaspoon Tabasco sauce • ¼ teaspoon black pepper, freshly ground

In fry pan, sauté onions in oil, add oregano, basil, and garlic. Add celery and green pepper and reduce heat to simmer until vegetables are cooked, about 5 minutes. Transfer to stockpot and add crumbled jerky, V8, chili powder, black beans, chickpeas, kidney beans, tomatoes (crush, if necessary), Tabasco, and pepper. Simmer, uncovered, for at least 1 hour. Serve over cooked potatoes or pasta, if desired.

SPAGHETTI

This recipe is my answer for any failed jerky. Cut the strips into small pieces or break up the ground meat jerkies with your fingers. Serves 6 to 8.

2 cups jerky, various-sized pieces

8 cups canned tomatoes • ½ cup dried mushrooms • 2 teaspoons dried basil • 2 teaspoons dried oregano • ½ teaspoon celery seed • 1 teaspoon fennel seeds, crushed • 2 tablespoons olive oil • 2 cups onion, chopped • 1 cup pepper, chopped • 1 teaspoon brown sugar • 1 tablespoon garlic, minced • spaghetti noodles • 1 cup Parmesan cheese

Put jerky in a bowl. Purée 4 cups of canned tomatoes and add to jerky. Add mushrooms, basil, oregano, celery seed, and fennel. Put olive oil in a large saucepan and sauté the onions and pepper. Add brown sugar and garlic. Stir and let sit. Return to heat and add the remaining 4 cups of canned tomatoes. Cook noodles and add sauce to spaghetti. Top with cheese.

JERKY BEANS

My husband, Joe, is the bean-maker in our family. He learned about a special dried corn called *chicos* while attending cooking classes in Santa Fe, New Mexico. Feel free to substitute any corn for chicos. Serves 8.

1 cup ham jerky, cut in ½-inch cubes

4 cups water • 2 cups dry red beans • 1 cup chicos • 1 cup onion, chopped • 2 teaspoons salt • 1 teaspoon cumin • 1 teaspoon black pepper • ½ teaspoon green chili powder • ½ teaspoon red chili powder

Sort and discard any imperfect beans. Wash. Cover and soak overnight in water. Drain, rinse with fresh water, and drain again. This presoaking tones the gas down. Place water in a kettle and add jerky, beans, and chicos. Bring to a boil and reduce heat to moderate, cover, and cook until the beans are tender, then add the spices.

JERKED RICE

It's easy: cook jerky with the rice. Once cooked, it makes a great base for adding bell pepper chunks, diced radishes, and shredded carrots. Then top with cheese. We like bleached, long-grain balsamic rice because it absorbs water, cooks faster, and is more easily digestible. This recipe can be taken along with adventuring in the outdoors. It is also great to top with a fried egg. Serves 4.

1 cup jerky, cut in small pieces

½ cup water • ½ cup dried kale, crushed • 2 tablespoons dried tomato pieces • 1 teaspoon onion powder • 1 teaspoon garlic powder • ¼ teaspoon dried basil • ¼ teaspoon dried oregano • 1 tablespoon olive oil • 3½ cups water • 2 cups long-grain brown rice • diced or shredded fresh vegetables, optional • ½ cup hard cheese, grated

Combine the first nine ingredients, stir, and let sit 30 minutes. Put water and rice in a cooker and add the other ingredients. Stir. Cook. Add optional fresh vegetables and top with cheese.

JERKY BREAD

Odessa Piper from L'Etoile restaurant in Madison, Wisconsin, developed a jerky croissant for the Saturday Madison Farmers' Market and I thought it was a great idea. For this recipe, use either a box of commercial bread dough mix or your own recipe.

½ cup jerky, chopped into ¼-inch pieces

1 loaf raw bread dough • ⅓ cup water • 1 tablespoon dried tomato pieces • 1 tablespoon dried onion pieces • 1 tablespoon dried carrots, shredded • 1 teaspoon dried basil • ½ teaspoon black pepper, finely ground • 1 teaspoon butter

Mix dough. In a small bowl, mix all the other ingredients minus the dough and the butter. Stir and let sit at least 15 minutes. When everything is sufficiently rehydrated, discard the rehydration liquid and knead into the dough. Place in an oiled baking tin and bake in a preheated 350-degree oven. When the crust is brown, remove from the oven, spread butter on the top, and set aside to cool.

CORN BREAD

While experimenting with drying jerky over a woodstove, my friend Sarah shared her favorite corn bread recipe. I experimented with it and added the jerky.

½ cup small jerky pieces

2 cups buttermilk • 1½ cup canola oil • 2 eggs, beaten • 1 teaspoon baking soda • 1 teaspoon salt • 2 cups flour • 1 cup cornmeal • 6 teaspoons baking powder

Put jerky in a bowl with 1 cup buttermilk. In a separate bowl, whisk the remaining ingredients, including the 1 cup reserved buttermilk, together. When well blended, stir in the rehydrated jerky and buttermilk. Bake in a greased 9-by-13-inch pan at 375 degrees for 25 to 30 minutes or until a toothpick comes out clean.

SALMON JERKY LOAFETTES

Adeline Deden, my mother-in-law, talked about making this salmon loaf recipe with her mother. Adeline was a creative and adventurous cook who jumped at the chance to make this recipe using dried salmon. Honeyed Salmon Jerky (page 86) is perfect with this recipe. Serves 6.

1 cup Honeyed Salmon Jerky, broken into ½-inch pieces

½ cup milk • 2 beaten eggs • 2 tablespoons melted butter • ½ cup cracker crumbs • 2 tablespoons chopped fresh parsley • ¼ teaspoon salt • ¼ teaspoon black pepper, freshly ground

Put jerky pieces in milk and let sit at least 30 minutes. Add remaining ingredients. Spoon into six greased cupcake forms or bake in a greased loaf pan or casserole dish. Bake 20 minutes at 350 degrees. Cool and serve with sauce.

SALMON LOAFETTE SAUCE

This sauce is wonderful. Try it over cooked potatoes. Serves 6.

2 tablespoons butter • 4 tablespoons chopped onion • 2 tablespoons flour • 1 cup half-and-half • 1 cup milk • 1 cup frozen peas, thawed • 1 tablespoon mushroom pieces

Melt butter and add onion. Cook until onion is translucent. Add flour. Stir. Add half-and-half and milk. Stir over medium heat until thickened. Add peas and mushrooms. Serve over baked Salmon Jerky Loafettes.

HOW ABOUT A JERKY PARTY?

JERKY CAKE

When I told a friend I wanted to include a recipe for jerky cake in this book, she said I'd lost my marbles. Well, maybe so, but it was a hit at my grandson's birthday party. How about a chocolate jerky cake? Fruity Jerky (page 66) is a good choice, but grind when it's cold, because at room temperature, it will be sticky and too difficult. Serves 12.

½ cup dried jerky, coarsely powdered

1 (16.75-ounce) box 1-step angel food cake mix

Make angel food cake according to instructions on box. After the cake is completely blended, fold in the jerky powder. Stir only enough to thoroughly mix. Bake according to box directions. Allow cake to cool before frosting.

JERKY FROSTING

What's a cake without frosting? My mom's answer was: "It's sweet bread."

2 tablespoons jerky, coarsely powdered

1 (7.2-ounce) package fluffy white frosting

Follow frosting box directions. Once frosting is completely mixed, add jerky. Frost cake and dribble shredded jerky over the top, as though you're using shredded chocolate or coconut.

JERKY ICE CREAM

This was inspired by the Peppercorn Ice Cream we tasted at L'Etoile Restaurant in Madison, Wisconsin. I've tried this with Hot Jerky strips and with custard and ice cream. What's most interesting is that it's both cold and hot at the same time. Serves 4 to 6.

2 tablespoons jerky, finely ground

2 tablespoons amaretto • ¼ teaspoon black peppercorns, finely ground

Mix these three ingredients together and let rehydrate at least 15 minutes.

Basic ice cream

1½ cups whole milk • 1⅛ cups white sugar • 3 cups heavy cream • 2 tablespoons vanilla extract

Combine milk and sugar and stir until the sugar dissolves. Stir in cream and vanilla. Add rehydrated jerky mixture and blend well. Then freeze.

OR

Place store-bought ice cream or custard in a larger container that has a lid that fits tight. Use a knife to cut the ice cream into small pieces. Add jerky and pepper and stir vigorously. Cover the container and immediately place in the freezer. Serve in small tablespoon dollops with fresh fruit or the frosted jerky cake.

CAMPING WITH JERKY

I was pretty young when I started backpacking and soon learned the benefits of taking dehydrated foods along when adventuring in the great outdoors. Dried foods more than lighten our load; they provide a way to have great food that nourishes our bodies as we breathe fresh air and experience the wonders of nature. Not only do we snack on great jerky, but we use it in cooking, too.

John Kvasnicka, past executive director of the Minnesota Deer Hunters Association, told about how, "Four weekends a year, eleven members of our family get together for campouts and cook over an open pit. We think of these outings as experiential learning where we reach consensus and peace of mind as a family. We're always more likely to reflect around a campfire with a piece of jerky in hand. In fact, I have yet to be in a camp where people do not like jerky—it's a staff of life, like bread and water.

"We've made jerky from wild turkey, bear, pheasant, antelope, deer, goose, moose, and elk. When you make it yourself, it's one of those foods that brings you closer to nature and connects you to your ancestors, who survived by living off the land."

A UNIQUE INDIVIDUAL

Verlen Krueger, at age eighty, was still an adventurer extraordinaire, a world-class canoeist, and an inspiration. What is truly amazing is that Verlen didn't step into a canoe until he was forty-one years old. After that, he canoed more than 100,000 miles, perhaps more than anyone else in the world. He canoed over 28,000 miles across the North American continent, went up and down the Mississippi River, and paddled from the Arctic Ocean to South America's Cape Horn. Verlen is one of the only people who canoed up the Grand Canyon—not down—up!

I heard about Verlen when he called to buy one of my books on dry supplies for his pending trip to canoe the full length of the Yukon River. This was a 2,040-mile trip from Whitehorse to the Bering Sea.

"For a canoeist or any adventurer, jerky speaks for itself," Verlen said. "It's lightweight, full of protein, doesn't break up in your pack, and keeps a long time. When it's vacuum packed, it won't give off a scent for bears or other wildlife and that's a good thing."

Verlen recalled an incredible jerky-making experience while on one of his canoe trips. "We were heading to Alaska and were way up in the Northwest Territories and had just portaged up the Richardson

Mountain, paddled through a pass, and come down a small creek. We'd made camp in a willow thicket along the sandy riverside and had just set up our tents. We had a fire going when we saw movements in the brush, near our campsite.

"It was a moose!" he said. "It was completely unaware of us, but our guide, a Native American for whom moose are always in season, prepared to shoot. We tried to talk him out of it and suggested there'd be too much wasted meat. But he shot. His aim was true and we spent the rest of the night butchering. The next morning, we filled our two canoes with meat and paddled to the nearest village to trade moose meat for groceries. With the meat we kept, we cut long thin strips about ¼ inch thick, rubbed the strips with salt and pepper, and began making jerky over our campfire. Drying all that moose meat took three nights. We'd dry it over the campfire at night, then the next morning we'd wrap it up as we traveled during the day, then hang it to dry again at night.

"It tasted great," he recalled. "Since then, I love moose meat. It's better than steak, but it's hard to get. I'll probably never have it that fresh again, since I don't carry a gun on my trips and I'm usually too busy canoeing to hunt or fish."

On this trip along the voyageurs' fur trade route, he canoed 6,000 miles from Montreal to the Bering Sea and encountered native people drying fish in preparation for the long Arctic winter. When the four canoeists arrived in the Northwest Territories, just above the Arctic Circle, after the long days of the Arctic midsummer, which happened to be during the salmon run, they spotted racks of fish drying along the riverbanks.

"We were curious and stopped to talk with the people and they told us that, as far back as they knew, their people had caught and dried fish in exactly the same way." To catch salmon, they used a fish wheel that had spokes that were placed over the river, and as the paddle turned, it dipped through the water and the spokes trapped the salmon and a bucket dumped the fish into another container. The fish were slit open and the innards were scraped out. The whole fish was left intact, including the skin and head. They were then hung on racks near a fire so that the smoke did the drying.

Verlen recalled, "I was surprised that it tasted more smoky than salty."

Since that experience, Verlen always took dried fish along on his wilderness adventures. "Dried fish help balance our carb-heavy diet," he said. "It was so great to get that dried fish because we didn't have time to waste fishing. We were concentrating on canoeing, because we wanted to do the entire route in one season because this had never been done before. It took the voyageurs two seasons to complete this route."

Drying fish in 1912.

VERLEN'S MAC 'N' CHEESY JERKY

In addition to eating jerky as a snack, Verlen used it in cooking. After setting up camp and building a good fire, he'd make his all-time favorite. Serves 2 to 4.

½ cup jerky, cut in small pieces

3 cups water • 2 cups macaroni noodles • 1 cup powdered cheese

Rehydrate the jerky. Then cook the macaroni until it's tender, then drain. Stir in cheese and add jerky.

DRIED GROUND MEAT

Although this is not really jerky, you can dry ground meat to take with you when adventuring away from home. This flavorful, high-protein, lightweight food really pays off when you arrive at your destination and add it to a pot of spaghetti.

You can flavor the ground meat during or after the cooking process.

One pound of fresh ground meat will become 4 to 6 ounces when dried and measure a little over 1 cup.

1 pound ground meat

2 tablespoons onion, finely chopped • 1 tablespoon bell pepper, finely chopped • 1 tablespoon Worcestershire sauce • 1 teaspoon garlic, minced • ½ teaspoon dried basil • ¼ teaspoon black pepper, freshly ground

Fry raw ground meat until it is well cooked, add remaining ingredients if pre-seasoning, remove from heat, and drain off the fat. Or put it in a colander and rinse oil off with hot water. Or spread the cooked meat over paper towels and press down with your hands. Or use a rolling pin to push any oil out of the meat. Place on roll-up sheets and dry.

THE ULTIMATE TRAIL MIX

What more could you want—jerky, salted nuts, and pickles? This combination has been a unanimous hit. Cut sweet or dill pickles into ¼- to ½-inch pieces, put in a dehydrator, and dry until chewy. Feel free to vary any of these ingredients with any kind of jerky. Makes 6 cups.

2 cups jerky, cut in ½-inch pieces

2 cups sweet, salty nuts • 1 cup dried pickle pieces • 1 cup salted sunflower seeds • 1 cup pumpkin seeds • 1 cup dried coconut, shredded • ¼ cup sesame seeds

Mix all ingredients together.

HAM JERKY WITH NOODLES

Judy Lynch says this "Wow!" meal can feed six hungry horseback riders. Even though cowboys are tough and don't mind carrying heavy Dutch ovens and iron frying pans, this is an easier way to enjoy a delicious meal while on the trail. Serves 4 to 6.

In Bag 1 put

4 cups ham jerky, cut in small cubes • 2 tablespoons chicken or turkey jerky, powdered • 2 teaspoons dried onions, minced

In Bag 2 put

¼ cup flour • 2 teaspoons curry powder • ½ teaspoon pepper

In Bag 3 put

2 cups powdered milk

In Bag 4 put

8 ounces noodles • ½ teaspoon salt

In Bag 5 put

1 cup Parmesan cheese, grated

In small container put

¼ cup butter

Label the five self-sealing plastic bags with the following list of ingredients and bring along. Put butter in a plastic container that has a tight seal. Place all five bags along with the butter container in one 2-gallon sealable plastic bag that's labeled "Ham with Noodles."

At camp: Pour contents of Bag 1 into a bowl and add 4 cups water. Let rehydrate at least 30 minutes. Drain off and save any excess liquid. Add enough additional water to make 4 cups. In another pot, boil water, add contents of Bag 4, then stir, cover, and remove from heat so the noodles can plump up.

For the sauce, melt butter in a large pot and add the ingredients from Bag 2. Stir and add the 4 cups of rehydration liquid and whisk until it thickens. Stir constantly and add the contents of Bag 3. Cook over low heat and then add contents of Bag 5 and Bag 1. Stir. Combine the sauce and noodles and serve immediately.

BACKPACKER CREAMED JERKY

For variety, add dried mushroom pieces to the rehydrating jerky. When you add more dried foods to any recipe, you may need to increase the rehydration liquid. Serves 2 to 4.

1 cup jerky, cut into small pieces

1 tablespoon dried pepper pieces • 1 tablespoon dried onions, minced • 2 tablespoons butter • 1 tablespoon flour • 1 cup cold water • ⅓ cup powdered milk • ¼ cup Parmesan cheese, grated • ½ teaspoon black pepper, freshly ground

Rehydrate jerky and dried vegetables in a saucepan with 1 cup water for at least 15 minutes. Bring to a boil for 5 minutes, taking care that the liquid doesn't completely evaporate. Remove jerky and vegetables from pan and put in a bowl. Melt butter and add flour, then brown the butter and flour. Stir constantly to prevent scorching. Mix water and powdered milk. Add milk to flour. Stir. Cook over low heat until thickened. Add jerky and vegetables and continue stirring. Remove from heat. Add cheese and pepper.

BACKPACKER COUNTRY SOUP

We started making this soup many years ago when we backpacked in the Big Horn Mountains. As a family, we always looked forward to this healthy and hearty meal. While at home, we put all the following ingredients in one package. Serves 4.

2 cups jerky pieces

1 cup dried potato chunks • ½ cup dried tomato, broken into pieces • ½ cup dried onions • ½ cup dried mushrooms • ¼ cup dried bell pepper pieces • 1 teaspoon salt • 1 teaspoon garlic • ¼ teaspoon powdered dried sage • ¼ teaspoon black pepper, freshly ground • ¼ teaspoon cayenne pepper • 1 bay leaf

When in camp, put 4 cups water and the dry soup mix in a pot and rehydrate at least 30 minutes. Remember that warm water speeds rehydration. Slowly bring to a boil over medium heat. Stir, cover, remove from heat, and let sit an additional 15 to 30 minutes. Add more water if necessary. Cover and cook over medium heat until all ingredients become soft. Remove bay leaf.

BACKPACKER GOULASH

While at home, prepare the goulash on page 144, but leave out jerky and do not add macaroni. Once cooked, spread the mixture evenly on lightly oiled roll-up sheets and place in a dehydrator until thoroughly dry. Store in airtight bags. Label with name and date. This should weigh 4 ounces dried and measure about 2 cups. Store jerky in one plastic bag and macaroni in another. Serves 2.

½ cup jerky, cut in small pieces

4 cups water • 2 cups dried goulash • 1 cup uncooked shell or elbow macaroni

Tear dried goulash into l-inch pieces. Soak dried goulash and jerky pieces in 2 cups water at least 30 minutes. In a separate pan, bring 2 cups water to a boil over medium-high heat and add macaroni. Once jerked goulash has rehydrated, cook over medium heat until excess liquid evaporates. Stir occasionally. Add drained, cooked macaroni, stir, cover, and remove from heat and enjoy.

Appendix: Jerky Pet Treats

One thing I learned from collecting stories is that licensing for pet treats was a lot simpler than licensing for human jerky consumption. I got so enthusiastic after talking with friend Stephanie Marcoux that I started making and selling my own 100 percent organic turkey breast treats that I called Gobbles.

"GRRR . . . MET"

Stephanie Marcoux's advice to anyone who has an idea and passion is, "Don't give up too soon. Persistence pays off."

Driving home from a job she hated, she heard herself making loud, deep-throated, growling sounds. "GRRRRRR!" she growled. Suddenly she remembered a conversation she'd with a friend, who had said somewhat flippantly, "Why don't you just sell those dog treats you make for Boots?"

"That's it!" she said to herself, "And I'll call my business, GRRR." Over time, her business name evolved to GRRRMET and the sound of freedom still resonates for Stephanie.

In the state of Washington, all she needed was a twenty-dollar business license, insurance, and to make sure her labels clearly state that her products were "For Pets."

Stephanie started to specialize in creating jerkies to satisfy specific pet needs and found a ready market. For example, a friend's dog was allergic to beef so she created a chicken breast jerky. Then for a special cat treat, she marinated chicken strips in garlic and Vietnamese anchovy extract. "Its fishiness appeals to cats," she said. After marinating for 3 hours, she dried the chicken until hard and then broke it into little pieces. "That is what cats prefer," she stated firmly.

"We cut everything by hand. I want nice ⅛-inch uniform strips. We don't use any chemicals or preservatives in any of our marinades." Stephanie uses round for her beef treats and marinates the strips in light soy sauce, honey, and garlic for 3 hours. She experimented with drying beef and chicken liver and found that "frozen liver was a disaster because it turned to mush when it thawed," she recalled. "Beef liver becomes a shiny, dark brown when it dries," she said. "Beware the smell of liver drying—it generates a very strong smell."

When a holistic practitioner told her that emu was good for animals with allergies, she found a local emu rancher. "Both dogs and cats go wild for small pieces of dried shrimp and calamari [squid], too."

"I have lots of stories about how much cats and dogs love my treats," she said. Her favorite is one about a cat owner who woke during the night when she heard dragging sounds across her wooden floor. The cat owner sat up in bed and thought she saw her husband's pants traveling across the floor. Thinking she must be dreaming, she lay down and went back to sleep. In the morning, the pants were in the hall, the pocket was inside out, and an empty shredded bag of GRRRMET treats was strewn about. Her husband had stuffed a package of calamari treats in his pocket, the cat crawled in, moved the pants across the floor and out of sight of the owner, and devoured the treats. Stephanie laughed, "That proves that calamari jerky is irresistible. It does smell pretty fishy."

I received inspiration from Stephanie in another way—she was one of the first people that creatively added other foods to her ground meat pet treats. Her husband, a mailman, refused to carry spray and instead he filled his pockets full of Jerky Puffs. The chicken, beef, and lamb puffs—his brain-child—are crunchy, round pet treats about the size of a melon ball.

To make the puffs, after cleaning the meat, they grind it only enough so that it's still a little chunky. The lamb puffs are made from leg of lamb, cooked brown rice, shredded raw carrots, and a little sea salt, and vegetable bouillon provides enough moisture to hold the puffs together. Chicken and beef puffs contain cooked white rice, shredded raw carrots, sea salt, and bouillon. Stephanie mixes the ingredients together, uses a melon baller as a scoop, then dries these little balls.

Her business not only served as inspiration, but her efforts also resulted in making a lot of pets and their owners very happy.

Note: Sad to say, my state of Minnesota is not as liberal as Washington and my little pet treat business did not survive because of bureaucratic constraints.

Jerky Pet Treats

Here are some hints about making jerky pet treats.

Cats are carnivores and they want meat. They love dried fish, calamari, shrimp, chicken, and turkey. Dogs are omnivores and can survive on plants, but they really enjoy beef, bison, lamb, turkey, and chicken. Pets should not have chocolate, onions, raisins, grapes, or macadamia nuts. Avoid adding yeast, minimize dairy products, and keep garlic and salt to a minimum.

Grind flavored or unflavored meats (or use narrow strips, if desired) and dry on leather sheets at 155 degrees. When dry, sprinkle on your pet's regular food. Cats like small pieces. Dogs don't care. Generally three pounds of fresh ground meat dries to about 1 pound.

Cat portion	½ to 1 teaspoon
Small dog	1 teaspoon
Medium-sized dog	1 tablespoon
Large dog	2 tablespoons

Metric Conversion Charts

METRIC AND IMPERIAL CONVERSIONS

(These conversions are rounded for convenience)

Ingredient	Cups/Tablespoons/ Teaspoons	Ounces	Grams/Milliliters
Butter	1 cup=16 tablespoons= 2 sticks	8 ounces	230 grams
Cream cheese	1 tablespoon	0.5 ounce	14.5 grams
Cheese, shredded	1 cup	4 ounces	110 grams
Cornstarch	1 tablespoon	0.3 ounce	8 grams
Flour, all-purpose	1 cup/1 tablespoon	4.5 ounces/0.3 ounce	125 grams/8 grams
Flour, whole wheat	1 cup	4 ounces	120 grams
Fruit, dried	1 cup	4 ounces	120 grams
Fruits or veggies, chopped	1 cup	5 to 7 ounces	145 to 200 grams
Fruits or veggies, pureed	1 cup	8.5 ounces	245 grams
Honey, maple syrup, or corn syrup	1 tablespoon	.75 ounce	20 grams
Liquids: cream, milk, water, or juice	1 cup	8 fluid ounces	240 ml
Oats	1 cup	5.5 ounces	150 grams
Salt	1 teaspoon	0.2 ounces	6 grams
Spices: cinnamon, cloves, ginger, or nutmeg (ground)	1 teaspoon	0.2 ounce	5 ml
Sugar, brown, firmly packed	1 cup	7 ounces	200 grams
Sugar, white	1 cup/1 tablespoon	7 ounces/0.5 ounce	200 grams/12.5 grams
Vanilla extract	1 teaspoon	0.2 ounce	4 grams

OVEN TEMPERATURES

Fahrenheit	Celsius	Gas Mark
225°	110°	¼
250°	120°	½
275°	140°	1
300°	150°	2
325°	160°	3
350°	180°	4
375°	190°	5
400°	200°	6
425°	220°	7
450°	230°	8

Photo Credits

Illustrations by Dale Mann: viii, xi, xiii, xv, 1, 5, 6, 9, 11, 13, 35, 47, 49, 131
Photos by Joe Deden: xiv, xv, xvi, 10, 15, 18, 30, 32, 48, 51, 57, 65, 100, 104, 105, 106, 114, 115, 131, 132, 134, 137, 139, 143, 146, 158
iStock: 36, 38, 45, 54, 55, 56, 60, 63, 64, 66, 67, 68, 69, 70, 72, 73, 75, 77, 83, 86, 89, 99, 102, 107, 108, 109, 110, 111, 112, 113, 116, 117, 118, 119, 125, 127, 133, 138, 140, 141, 145, 147, 148, 149, 150, 151, 152, 153, 154, 155, 157, 161, 164, 166, 170

8: Courtesy of Nesco

12: Ira Newman

16: Second to None Meats - Bison and Elk Jerky by Calgary Reviews
     (cc) BY
     www.flickr.com/photos/calgaryreviews/5923963153

23: Sean Broadnax

25: "Oh Boy! Oberto" *Miss Madison Unlimited* Hydroplane by Clemens Vasters (cc) BY
     www.flickr.com/photos/clemensv/11112511593/in/photostream

43: Doug Care Equipment website

53: Syrup grades large by Dvortygirl (cc) BY-SA
     commons.wikimedia.org/wiki/File:Syrup_grades_large.JPG

58: Courtesy of Nesco

59: Myers's Original Dark Rum 40% by Dominic Lockyer (cc) BY-SA
     www.flickr.com/photos/farehamwine/14718793500/in/photolist-oqDEvJ-izWEcx

61: Johnnie Walker Splash by Friedrich Böhringer (cc) BY-SA
     ommons.wikimedia.org/wiki/File:Johnnie_Walker_Splash.JPG

62: Fountain Soda by National Cancer Institute (S) PUBLIC DOMAIN
     commons.wikimedia.org/wiki/File:FountainSoda.jpg

76: Limes by Daderot (S) PUBLIC DOMAIN
     commons.wikimedia.org/wiki/File:Limes_-_DSC06056.JPG

79: Wild Turkey by Zion National Park (cc) BY
www.flickr.com/photos/54168808@N03/6384983627

82: Trout by Jonathunder (cc) BY-SA
commons.wikimedia.org/wiki/File:Trout.jpg

84: Taku Smokeries website

85: Salmon Sashimi Close up by Kyoto Kenshu (cc) BY-SA
commons.wikimedia.org/wiki/File:Salmon_sashimi_close_up.jpg

91: Mary T. Bell

92: Ameiurus melas by Duane Raver from U.S. Fish and Wildlife Service
(cc) PUBLIC DOMAIN
commons.wikimedia.org/wiki/File:Ameiurus_melas_by_Duane_
Raver.png

97: Courtesy of Nesco

98: Courtesy of Nesco

101: Sekaná by Matěj Baťha (cc) BY-SA
commons.wikimedia.org/wiki/File:Sekaná_005.jpg

120: Kümmel by Slick (cc) PUBLIC DOMAIN
commons.wikimedia.org/wiki/File:Kümmel_2012–07–08–9523.jpg

121: Mint-leaves-2007 by Kham Tran (cc) BY
commons.wikimedia.org/wiki/File:Mint-leaves-2007.jpg

122: Pineapple – small pieces by Mattes (cc) BY-SA
commons.wikimedia.org/wiki/File:Pineapple_-_small_pieces.JPG

124: Cyprinus carpio by Dezidor (cc) BY-SA
commons.wikimedia.org/wiki/File:Cyprinus_carpio.jpeg

135: Two yellow organically grown plums on tree in plum orchard (cc) PUBLIC DOMAIN
www.public-domain-image.com/free-images/flora-plants/fruits/
plums-fruit-pictures/two-yellow-organically-grown-plums-on-tree-in-
plum-orchard

136: Bruehe 2 by Rainer Zens (cc) BY-SA
commons.wikimedia.org/wiki/File:Bruehe-2.jpg

156: Frozen peas by Jina Lee (cc) BY-SA
en.wikipedia.org/wiki/File:Frozen_peas.JPG

159: Pestle and Mortar with peppercorns by Gisela Francisco (cc) BY
commons.wikimedia.org/wiki/File:Pestle_and_Mortar_with_pepper-
corns.jpg

163: Drying fish by C. G. Linde [🆔 PUBLIC DOMAIN]
commons.wikimedia.org/wiki/File:Drying_fish_(HS85–10–26193).jpg

165: Cooking beef by Andrew Bossi [cc BY-SA]
commons.wikimedia.org/wiki/File:2008_04_23_-_Laurel_-_Cooking_beef_1.JPG

168: Dried mushrooms by André Karwath [cc BY-SA]
commons.wikimedia.org/wiki/File:Dried_mushrooms.jpg

Recipe Index

Notes